THE BRITANNICA GUIDE TO
THE VISUAL AND PERFORMING ARTS

THE HISTORY OF
WESTERN
ARCHITECTURE

EDITED BY
NATASHA C. DHILLON

Britannica®
Educational Publishing
IN ASSOCIATION WITH

ROSEN
EDUCATIONAL SERVICES

First Edition

Britannica Educational Publishing
J.E. Luebering: Director, Core Reference Group
Anthony L. Green: Editor, Compton's by Britannica

Rosen Publishing
Hope Lourie Killcoyne: Executive Editor
Natasha C. Dhillon: Editor
Nelson Sá: Art Director
Michael Moy: Designer
Cindy Reiman: Photography Manager

Library of Congress Cataloging-in-Publication Data

The history of Western architecture/Edited by Natasha C. Dhillon.—First Edition.
    pages cm.—(The Britannica guide to the visual and performing arts)
Includes bibliographical references and index.
ISBN 978-1-68048-088-7 (library bound)
1. Architecture—History—Juvenile literature. I. Dhillon, Natasha C., editor.
NA200.H57 2015
720.9—dc23

2014044538

Manufactured in the United States of America

Photo credits: Cover, p. i DEA/X. Desmier/De Agostini/Getty Images; p. ix pcruciatti/Shutterstock.com; p. 3 Dan Breckwoldt/Shutterstock.com; pp. 9, 33, 43 Encyclopædia Britannica, Inc.; p. 13 © Corbis; pp. 18–19 zebra0209/Shutterstock.com; p. 23 © Pierdelune/Shutterstock.com; p. 27 Evgeny Shmulev/Shutterstock.com; p. 30 airphoto.gr/Shutterstock.com; pp. 36–37 Circumnavigation/Shutterstock.com; p. 51 Bartosz Turek/Shutterstock.com; pp. 56–57 junjun/Shutterstock.com; p. 63 Nick_Nick/Shutterstock.com; p. 65 DEA/S.Vannini/De Agostini/Getty Images; p. 70 Attilios; p. 75 Isantilli/Shutterstock.com; p. 81 G. Berengo Gardin/© DeA Picture Library; p. 90 Tips Images/SuperStock; p. 95 © Thomas M. Perkins/Shutterstock.com; p. 100 © c/Fotolia; pp. 106–107, 165 Claudio Divizia/Shutterstock.com; p. 111 © 1997, AISA, Archivo Iconográfico, Barcelona, España; pp. 118–119 Baloncici/Shutterstock.com; p. 137 © Tupungato/Shutterstock.com; p. 142 © David Gee 4/Alamy; p. 153 Kanuman/Shutterstock.com; p. 156 © Wayne Andrews/Esto; p. 160 © Dainis Derics/Shutterstock.com; p. 181 Walter Bibikow/AWL Images/Getty Images; p. 196 © robepco/Fotolia; p. 197 fotog/Getty Images; p. 199 © Pierre Faure/Fotolia; pp. 210–211 eXpose/Shutterstock.com; p. 218 Roy Luck/Flickr/flickr.com/photos/royluck/7379412070/CC BY 2.0; cover and interior pages graphic elements David M. Schrader/Shutterstock.com, E_K/Shutterstock.com, Valentin Agapov/Shutterstock.com, argus/Shutterstock.com, Iakov Filimonov/Shutterstock.com.

CONTENTS

By the simplest definition, architecture is the design of buildings executed by architects. However, it is more. It is the expression of thought in building. It is not simply construction, the piling of stones or the spanning of spaces with steel girders. It is the intelligent creation of forms and spaces that in themselves express an idea.

Building construction is an ancient human activity. It began with the purely functional need for a controlled environment to moderate the effects of climate. Constructed shelters were one means by which human beings were able to adapt themselves to a wide variety of climates and become a global species.

Human shelters were at first very simple and perhaps lasted only a few days or months. The hunter-gatherers of the late Stone Age, who moved about a wide area in search of food, built the earliest temporary shelters that appear in the archaeological record. A tent illustrates the basic elements of environmental

From left to right, 122 Leadenhall Street (the Cheesegrater), 30 St. Mary Axe (the Gherkin), and 20 Fenchurch Street (the Walkie Talkie), skyscrapers in London's financial district. In addition to serving a particular purpose, most notable works of architecture have a dramatic visual impact.

control that are the concern of building construction.

Over time, however, even temporary structures evolved into such highly refined forms as the igloo. Gradually more durable structures began to appear, particularly after the advent of agriculture, when people began to stay in one place for long periods. Some structures began to have symbolic as well as functional value, marking the beginning of the distinction between architecture and building.

Construction becomes intelligent and thus architectural when it is efficient and immediately appears so. If it is the simplest and most advanced type of structure, solving the task set for it, and conceivable in its age, construction will have the quality of perfect appropriateness and will also be the expression of the mechanical knowledge of a culture. It becomes intelligent also when it is made to emphasize its simplicity and to express its system of support so that both can be immediately understood.

The characteristics that distinguish a work of architecture from other man-made structures are (1) the suitability of the work to use by human beings in general and the adaptability of it to particular human activities, (2) the stability and permanence of the work's construction, and (3) the communication of experience and ideas through its form. All these conditions must be met in architecture. The second is a constant, while the first and third vary in relative importance according to the social function of buildings. If the function is chiefly utilitarian, as in a factory, communication is of less importance. If the function is chiefly expressive, as in a monumental tomb, utility is a minor concern. In some buildings, such as churches and city halls, utility and communication may be of equal importance.

Construction, however, only became a basic factor in architectural thought during the Roman era at the time of the birth of Christ.

Before then architecture had been almost exclusively symbolic in form and decoration. The symbols that were materialized in the Egyptian pyramid, Sumerian ziggurat, Hindu stupa, and Japanese pagoda were the most powerful expression of each culture's religious beliefs. They were designed according to the most complex and all-embracing symbolic systems; their shape, decoration, dimensions, and orientation to the sun were the result of the most profound meditation. But they enclosed little or no internal space. They were works of architecture but not of construction.

When intelligent, permanent construction enclosing space replaced the symbolic architecture of primitive cultures, a new type of architectural art appeared. It became possible for a whole city to become a work of architecture with each contributing element—places of worship, government institutions, markets, houses—enclosed in an appropriate structure and decorated to express its individual character.

The cities of Rome, Ravenna, Constantinople, and Isfahan became possible with their colourful domes, cavernous markets, and decorated palaces. Their interior spaces also became symbolic in their shape and decoration as seen in the Islamic mosque and in Byzantine and Gothic churches. Greek architecture was based chiefly on the post-and-beam system, with columns carrying the load. Timber construction was superseded by construction in marble and stone. The column, a unit human in scale, was used as a module for all of a temple's proportions. The Doric order, probably the earliest, remained the favourite of the Greek mainland and western colonies. The Ionic order developed in eastern Greece; on the mainland, it was used chiefly for smaller temples and interiors. Both Doric and Ionic orders are present in the Athens Acropolis, the greatest Greek architectural achievement. The Hellenistic Age produced more elaborate and richly decorated architecture, with often colossal buildings. Many of the great buildings were secular rather than religious, and the Ionic and especially the newer Corinthian orders were widely used.

The Romans used the Greek orders and added two new ones, Tuscan and Composite, but the Corinthian was by far the most popular. Roman architects used columns not only as functional bearing elements but also as applied (engaged) decoration. Though rigidly adhering to symmetry, the Romans used a variety of spatial forms. Whereas Greek temples were isolated and almost always faced east-west, Roman temples were oriented with respect to other buildings. The discovery of concrete enormously facilitated construction using the arch, vault, and dome, as in the Pantheon. Other public buildings included basilicas, baths, amphitheatres, and triumphal arches.

Byzantine architects were eclectic, at first drawing heavily on Roman temple features. Byzantine structures featured soaring spaces and sumptuous decoration: marble columns and inlay, mosaics on the vaults, inlaid-stone pavements, and sometimes gold coffered ceilings. The architecture of Constantinople extended throughout the Christian East and in some places, notably Russia, remained in use after the fall of Constantinople.

A fusion of Roman, Carolingian and Ottonian, Byzantine, and local Germanic traditions, Romanesque architecture was a product of the great expansion of monasticism in the 10th and 11th centuries. Larger churches were needed to accommodate the numerous monks and priests, as well as the pilgrims who came to view saints' relics. For the sake of fire resistance, masonry vaulting began to replace timber construction. Romanesque churches characteristically incorporated semicircular arches for windows, doors, and arcades; barrel or groin vaults to support the roof of the nave; massive piers and walls, with few windows, to contain the outward thrust of the vaults; side aisles with galleries above them; a large tower over the crossing of nave and transept; and smaller towers at the church's western end.

Gothic architecture lasted in Europe from the mid-12th century to the 16th century. It was a style of masonry building characterized by cavernous spaces with the expanse of walls broken up by overlaid tracery. In the 12th and 13th centuries, feats of engineering permitted increasingly gigantic buildings. The rib vault, flying buttress, and pointed (Gothic) arch were used as solutions to the problem of building a very tall structure while preserving as much natural light as possible. Stained-glass window panels rendered startling sun-dappled interior effects. The High Gothic years (*c.* 1250–1300), heralded by Chartres Cathedral, were dominated by France, especially with the development of the Rayonnant style. Britain, Germany, and Spain produced variations of this style, while Italian Gothic stood apart in its use of brick and marble rather than stone. Late Gothic (15th century) architecture reached its height in Germany's vaulted hall churches.

With the Renaissance in Europe around 1400, there came a new sort of architecture in which mass and interior space were manipulated to produce aesthetically pleasing pictures like those in paintings and sculptures. The elaborate symbolism of primitive and medieval art disappeared. In its place was a purely human-centred handling of form and space to produce visual delight.

There was a revival of ancient Roman forms, including the column and round arch, the tunnel vault, and the dome. The basic design element was the order. Knowledge of Classical architecture came from the ruins of ancient buildings and the writings of Vitruvius. As in the Classical period, proportion was the most important factor of beauty; Renaissance architects found a harmony between human proportions and buildings. This concern for proportion resulted in clear, easily compre-hended space and mass, which distinguishes the Renaissance style from the more complex Gothic. From Florence the early Renaissance style spread through Italy. Donato Bramante's move to Rome ushered in the High Renais-sance (*c.* 1500–20). Mannerism, the style of the Late Renaissance (1520–1600), was character-ized by sophistication, complexity, and novelty rather than the harmony, clarity, and repose of the High Renaissance. The Late Renaissance also saw much architectural theorizing.

During the Baroque period (*c.* 1600–1750), architecture, painting, and sculpture were integrated into decorative ensembles. Baroque architecture had its origins in the Counter-Reformation, when the Catholic Church launched an overtly emotional and sensory appeal to the faithful through art and architecture. Complex architectural plan shapes, often based on the oval, and the dynamic opposition and interpenetration of spaces were favoured to heighten the feeling of motion and sensuality. Other characteristic qualities include grandeur, drama and con-trast (especially in lighting), curvaceousness, and an often dizzying array of rich surface treatments, twisting elements, and gilded statuary. Architects unabashedly applied bright colours and illusory, vividly painted ceilings. Baroque buildings dominated their environment; Renaissance buildings separated themselves from it.

The late Baroque style is often referred to as Rococo. From France the Rococo style spread in the 1730s to the Catholic German-speaking lands, where it was adapted to a brilliant style of religious architecture that combined French elegance with south German fantasy as well as with a lingering Baroque interest in dramatic spatial and plastic effects. Some of the most beautiful of all Rococo buildings outside France are to be seen in Munich.

Neoclassical architecture was a revival of Classical architecture during the 18th and early 19th centuries. The movement concerned itself with the logic of entire Classical volumes, unlike Classical revivalism, which tended to reuse Classical parts. Neoclassical architecture is characterized by grandeur of scale, simplicity of geometric forms, Greek—especially Doric—or Roman detail, dramatic use of columns, and a preference for blank walls. The new taste for antique simplicity represented a general reaction to the excesses of the Rococo style. Neoclassicism thrived in the United States and Europe, with examples occurring in almost every major city. By 1800 nearly all new British architecture reflected the Neoclassical spirit. In the United States Neoclassicism continued to flourish throughout the 19th century, as many architects looked to make the analogy between the young country and imperial Rome when designing major government buildings. The style also spread to colonial Latin America.

Gothic revival drew its inspiration from medieval architecture and competed with the Neoclassical revivals in the United States and Great Britain. The first nostalgic imitation of Gothic architecture appeared in the 18th century, when scores of houses with castle-style battlements were built in England, but only toward the mid-19th century did a true Gothic Revival develop. The mere imitation of Gothic forms and details then became its least important aspect, as architects focused on creating original works based on underlying Gothic principles. Though the movement began losing force toward the end of the century, it was to remain one of the most potent and long-lived of the 19th-century revival styles.

The demystification of architecture during the Renaissance prepared the way for modern design. In the 19th century the picturesque—the design of both buildings and their landscape surroundings as if they were pictures—evolved. Enthusiasm for the picturesque evolved partly as a reaction against the earlier 18th-century trend of Neoclassicism, with its emphasis on formality, proportion, order, and exactitude. The term "picturesque" originally denoted a landscape scene that looked as if it came out of a painting in the style of the 17th-century French artists Claude Lorrain or Gaspard Poussin. The English architect and town planner John Nash produced some of the most exemplary works incorporating the concept.

By the beginning of the 20th century, architects also had increasingly abandoned past styles and conventions in favour of a form of architecture based on essential functional concerns. They were helped by advances in building technologies such as the steel frame and the curtain wall. In the period after World War I these tendencies became codified as the International Style, which utilized simple geometric shapes and unadorned facades and which abandoned any use of historical reference; the modernist steel-and-glass buildings of Ludwig Mies van der Rohe and Le Corbusier embodied this style. In the mid-to-late 20th century this style manifested itself in clean-lined, unadorned glass skyscrapers and mass housing projects.

Bauhaus—an influential, forward-looking German school of architecture and applied arts that was especially popular from 1919 to 1933—was founded by Walter Gropius with the ideal of integrating art, craftsmanship, and technology. Realizing that mass production had to be the precondition of successful design in the machine age, its members rejected the Arts and Crafts Movement's emphasis on individually executed luxury objects. The Bauhaus is often associated with a severe but elegant geometric style carried out with great economy of means, though in fact the works produced by its members were richly diverse.

In the 1960s some modification of the prevailing attitudes toward design of the previous 50 years began to take place. There was a revival of interest in traditional forms and historical styles. The U.S. architect Louis Kahn reacted to the abstraction in the works of Le Corbusier and Mies by using regular geometric compositions and materials such as brick, stone, and wood that made reference to the spirit of some of the architecture from the past, especially Egyptian, Greek, and Roman. Other architects rejected International Style modernism in more literal ways, using past forms like Classical columns or drawing on the architecture of modern popular culture, the highway, and the suburb for inspiration. This postmodernist artistic experimentation has run parallel to the explosion of construction for purely practical purposes.

New trends began to emerge at the close of the 20th century. Combining deconstruction's interest in tension and oppositions with the design vocabulary of Russian Constructivism, deconstructivist architects such as Frank Gehry challenged the functionalist aesthetic of modern architecture through designs using radical geometries, irregular forms, and complex, dynamic constructions. Into the 21st century, computer technology became a significant part of architectural design, allowing architects to envision new concepts and forms.

This volume traces the evolution of architecture through the ages, providing an overview of the myriad structures—historical, cultural, and functional—that have become so integral to urban, regional, and national landscapes both in the West and the world over.

CHAPTER ONE

ANCIENT ARCHITECTURE

Mankind first used indestructible materials to erect large structures not to live in but to worship their gods. From the beginning of settled habitation about 10,000 BCE to the rise of the Roman Empire, houses were built of the flimsiest materials and were not expected to outlast the lives of their inhabitants. A few early civilizations—especially the Assyrians, Persians, and Minoans—erected monumental palaces, but these were the residences of priest-kings. Architecture originated in the religious impulse and thus was originally symbolic.

The earliest permanent constructions consist of huge stones, roughly shaped, arranged in lines or circles. The one at Stonehenge in England is the best known of these complexes. The stones were set up by several successive peoples inhabiting the region between 3000 and 1600 BCE. They are grouped in four concentric circles, two of which are formed by paired uprights bearing huge capstones.

Because they are arranged to align with the sun at the summer and winter solstices, it is generally assumed that the complex served as a monumental calendar in which rites were performed on significant days of the year. Similar circles of stones were set up elsewhere in England, at Avebury most particularly, and in France at Carnac. Clusters of stones spanned by roof slabs, called dolmens, and single stones that stood on end, called menhirs, were also erected in large numbers, especially in Europe.

EGYPT

The Egyptian pyramids were far more sophisticated and larger in size but similar symbolically to the stone constructions of England and France for their use of sacred stones. The fertile Nile Valley permitted a civilization ruled by god-kings, the pharaohs, to develop there about 3000 BCE. The necessity of carrying out extensive irrigation projects meant that the Egyptians were organized to build on a large scale. Furthermore, the high limestone cliffs hemming in the valley provided an inexhaustible supply of fine building stone.

Royal tombs were built along the edges of cliffs, at first as low rectangular mastabas, then as tall four-sided pyramids. The earliest of the pyramids was that of the pharaoh Zoser erected at Saqqara about 2700–2600 BCE. Three huge pyramids built at Giza, near Cairo, about 2500 BCE, were the culmination of the series. The largest of these, the great pyramid of the pharaoh Cheops, measured 756 feet (230 metres) on a side at its base and was 481 feet (147 metres) high. In spite of its huge size, however, it

The pyramids of Giza were built to protect the tombs of pharaohs and other important individuals. Their shape symbolizes the rays of the sun reaching down to Earth as well as the path deceased pharaohs ascended to join the sun-god.

enclosed no space other than a narrow pas-
sage leading to a small tomb chamber in its
centre. It was constructed of limestone blocks,
each weighing between 3 and 15 tons, that
were piled one on top of the other.

The Egyptians worshipped the sun as
their chief god, often represented by a symbolic pyramidal stone, or *benben*. The Egyptian hieroglyph for the sun was a triangle
divided into three zones horizontally—red,
white, and yellow. It would seem to represent
the sun (the top, or yellow zone) spreading its
rays upon the Earth (the bottom, or red zone).
The pyramids at Giza were once faced in a
smooth coating of white marble with a band
of pink at the base and a pyramidal block of
pure gold at the top.

It has been concluded that the pyramids
themselves were huge benbens, symbols of the
sun and its rays reaching down to Earth. When
the pharaoh died he was said to ascend the
sun's rays to join his father, the sun-god. Thus
the pyramid would also seem to have been the
symbolic staircase up which its occupant, the
pharaoh, would climb to reach heaven.

To the east of Egypt another civilization appeared about 3000 BCE—that of the
Sumerians in the river valley of the Tigris and
Euphrates called Mesopotamia, or the "land
between the rivers." This too was a highly
organized culture capable of carrying out
large irrigation and construction projects. But

it differed from Egypt in two respects: it had no stone with which to build, only river clay, so that its architecture is entirely in brick; and it had no single divine ruler but was divided into a number of independent city-states and worshipped unseen gods.

SUMER

The Sumerian temple was a small brick house that the god was supposed to visit periodically. It was ornamented so as to recall the reed houses built by the earliest Sumerians in the valley. This house, however, was set on a brick platform, which became larger and taller as time progressed until the platform at Ur (built around 2100 BCE) was 150 by 200 feet (45 by 60 metres) and 75 feet (23 metres) high. These Mesopotamian temple platforms are called ziggurats, a word derived from the Assyrian *ziqquratu*, meaning "high." They were symbols in themselves; the ziggurat at Ur was planted with trees to make it represent a mountain. There the god visited Earth, and the priests climbed to its top to worship.

The ziggurat continued as the essential temple form of Mesopotamia during the later Assyrian and Babylonian eras. In these later times it became taller and more towerlike, perhaps with a spiral path leading up to the temple at the top. The Greek historian Herodotus wrote that the main temple of Babylon, the famous Tower of Babel, was such a tower divided into seven diminishing stages, each a different colour: white, black, purple, blue, orange, silver, and gold.

GREECE

The increased wealth of Greece in the 7th century BCE was enhanced by overseas trade and by colonizing activity in Italy and Sicily that had opened new markets and resources. Athens did not send out colonists and did not engage in vigorous trade, and it declined as a cultural and artistic centre. Corinth, Sparta, the islands, the cities of eastern Greece, and Crete came to the fore with their diverse artistic interests and means of expression. At no other time were there such strongly differentiated regional schools of art in the Greek world. The cities demonstrated their wealth and power, particularly in temple building, which was to foster new architectural forms, and also in the decoration of the temples and of the national sanctuaries. These architectural arts in turn encouraged imaginative and ambitious forms in sculpture and painting.

The greatest of the early religious types is the Greek temple, which evolved during the thousand years before the birth of Jesus. Until the age of Alexander the Great, the Greeks erected permanent stone buildings almost exclusively for religious monuments, like the Egyptians, Sumerians, and Hindus. Their temples were not large enclosures of space but statue chambers containing a god's sacred image. These chambers were accessible only to priests. Yet the Greek temple has always been seen as fundamentally distinct from and superior to most other early religious types, partly because of the simplicity of its form, partly because of the exquisite refinement of the best examples (especially the Parthenon on the Acropolis in Athens), and partly because it is seen to reflect the emergence in Greece of a rational, philosophical approach to art that replaced earlier belief systems.

THE "ORIENTALIZING" PERIOD

From about 650 on, the Greeks began to visit Egypt regularly, and their observation of the monumental stone buildings there was the genesis of the ultimate development of monumental architecture and sculpture in Greece. The first step in architecture was simply the replacement of wooden pillars with stone ones and the translation of the carpentry and brick structural forms into stone equivalents. This provided an opportunity for the expression of proportion and pattern, an expression that eventually took the form of the invention or evolution of the stone "orders" of architecture. These orders, or arrangements of specific types of columns supporting an upper section called an entablature, defined the pattern of the columnar facades and upperworks that formed the basic decorative shell of the Greek temple building.

There are two types of Greek temple: the Ionic, evolved in Ionia on the eastern shore of the Aegean Sea, and the Doric, evolved on the western shore. Their forms must originally have had symbolic meaning. Both show the same basic plan: a central windowless statue chamber, the cella; a porch, usually with two columns in front; and a ring of columns, the peristyle, around the four sides. The cella and porch seem to have been the original elements of the temple. They reproduce the primitive Greek house so that the god is symbolically depicted as living like a chief. The temple is usually set on a natural hill, or acropolis, but has no artificial platform beyond a three-step foundation, or stylobate. The peristyle was a later addition, apparently borrowed from the Egyptians, evidently to enlarge and ornament the symbolic god-house inside. A low, sloping roof tops the building with gables, called pediments, on the short sides.

The Ionic and Doric temples differ in their details. The Doric temple is simple in plan, the Ionic larger with a double peristyle. The columns differ: the Doric has a dish-shaped top, or capital, and no base, while the Ionic has paired volutes at its capital and carved rings at its base. The lintels, or entablatures, spanning the columns are also distinct, the Doric having a row of projecting blocks, or tri-glyphs, between sculpted metopes. The Ionic elements are smaller and taller, the Doric forms shorter and broader.

What is remarkable and unique about the Greek temple is the conscious adjustment

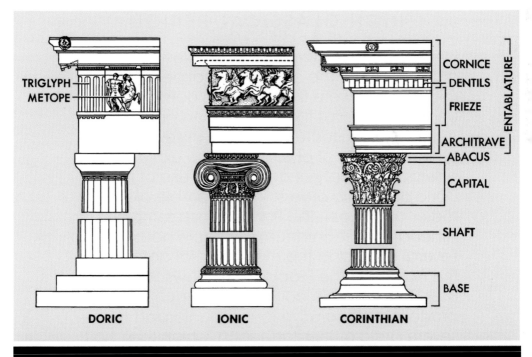

A comparison of the three main Greek column styles—Doric, Ionic, and Corinthian, the last exhibiting the most ornate capital of the three. Romans modified Greek orders to form two others—the Tuscan and the Composite.

of these orders by Greek architects for purely aesthetic effect. For the first time in history, architects, not priests, directed these building projects. Many of their names are known, and several wrote books about their aesthetic experiments. A book that has survived to the present is *De Architectura* ("On Architecture") by the Roman architect Marcus Vitruvius Pollio, who was active at the time of the birth of Christ. It is an authoritative source of information on much of Greek architectural theory and practice.

HIGH CLASSICAL PERIOD

By far the most impressive examples of Greek architecture of the high Classical period (*c.* 450–400 BCE) were the buildings constructed under Pericles for the Athenian Acropolis. The Acropolis architecture, which is in several ways a clear display of civic pride, also exhibits considerable subtlety of design in its use of the Doric and Ionic orders. The ensemble of the major buildings—the Parthenon, a temple to Athena; the Erechtheum, a temple housing several cults; and the monumental gateway to the Acropolis, the Propylaea—shows the orders used in deliberate contrast: the Erechtheum provides a decorative Ionic counterpart to the severe Doric of the Parthenon, which itself has an Ionic frieze; and in the Propylaea, columns of both orders complement each other.

Greek designers sought perfect orderliness in their rendition of the temple form. They adjusted the number of columns across the ends in relation to those down the sides. They aligned all the accents along the elevations so that each unit defined by one column (in the Doric order) was divided in the entablature into two triglyphs and metopes, four mutules under the cornice, four water spouts along the roof edge, and eight roof tiles. The most perfect example of this, the Parthenon in Athens, was built in 447–438 BCE by the architects Ictinus and Callicrates for the political leader Pericles.

Within this strictly ordered framework, the Greek architect worked to endow every part with interest and life in the carving of its surface. The spiral of the Ionic volute, the curve of the Doric capital, the depth and breadth of the flutes were varied endlessly for effect. The translucence and fine grain of the marble used in the most important buildings were an important help in making these refinements perceptible. Most amazing was the application of this work of adjustment to the temple as a whole, particularly in the case of the Parthenon. Here the stylobate and entablature are very slightly curved so that they rise in the centre of each side, while the columns are made to lean slightly inward—the angle increasing as they approach the corners— and the distance between the shafts varied. Nor are the column shafts themselves straight

PARTHENON

The Parthenon was the chief temple of the Greek goddess Athena on the hill of the Acropolis at Athens, Greece. It was built in the mid-5th century BCE and is generally considered to be the culmination of the development of the Doric order, the simplest of the three Classical Greek architectural orders. The name Parthenon refers to the cult of Athena Parthenos ("Athena the Virgin") that was associated with the temple.

Directed by the Athenian statesman Pericles, the Parthenon was built by the architects Ictinus and Callicrates under the supervision of the sculptor Phidias. Work began in 447 BCE, and the building itself was completed by 438. The same year a great gold and ivory statue of Athena, made by Phidias for the interior, was dedicated. Work on the exterior decoration of the building continued until 432 BCE.

Although the rectangular white marble Parthenon has suffered damage over the centuries, including the loss of most of its sculpture, its basic structure has remained intact. A colonnade of fluted, baseless columns with square capitals stands on a three-stepped base and supports an entablature, or roof structure, consisting

The remains of the Parthenon still stand on the hill of the Acropolis in Athens, Greece.

of a plain architrave, or band of stone; a frieze of alternating triglyphs (vertically grooved blocks) and metopes (plain blocks with relief sculpture, now partly removed); and, at the east and west ends, a low triangular pediment, also with relief sculpture (now mostly removed). The colonnade, consisting of 8 columns on the east and west and 17 on the north and

(continued on the next page)

(continued from the previous page)

south, encloses a walled interior rectangular chamber, or cella, originally divided into three aisles by two smaller Doric colonnades closed at the west end just behind the great cult statue. The only light came through the east doorway, except for some that might have filtered through the marble tiles in the roof and ceiling. Behind the cella, but not originally connected with it, is a smaller, square chamber entered from the west. The east and west ends of the interior of the building are each faced by a portico of six columns. Measured by the top step of the base, the building is 101.34 feet (30.89 metres) wide and 228.14 feet (69.54 metres) long.

The Parthenon embodies an extraordinary number of architectural refinements, which combine to give a plastic, sculptural appearance to the building. Among them are an upward curvature of the base along the ends and repeated in the entablature; an imperceptible, delicate convexity (entasis) of the columns as they diminish in diameter toward the top; and a thickening of the four corner columns to counteract the thinning effect of being seen at certain angles against the sky.

The sculpture decorating the Parthenon rivaled its architecture in careful harmony.

The metopes over the outer colonnade were carved in high relief and represented, on the east, a battle between gods and giants; on the south, Greeks and centaurs; and on the west, probably Greeks and Amazons. Those on the north are almost all lost. The continuous, low-relief frieze around the top of the cella wall, representing the annual Panathenaic procession of citizens honouring Athena, culminated on the east end with a priest and priestess of Athena flanked by two groups of seated gods. The pediment groups, carved in the round, show, on the east, the birth of Athena and, on the west, her contest with the sea god Poseidon for domination of the region around Athens. The entire work is a marvel of composition and clarity, which was further enhanced by colour and bronze accessories.

The Parthenon remained essentially intact until the 5th century CE, when Phidias' colossal statue was removed and the temple was transformed into a Christian church. By the 7th century, certain structural alterations in the inner portion had also been made. The Turks seized the Acropolis in 1458, and two years later they adopted the Parthenon as a mosque, without material change except for the

(continued on the next page)

(continued from the previous page)

raising of a minaret at the southwest corner. During the bombardment of the Acropolis in 1687 by Venetians fighting the Turks, a powder magazine located in the temple blew up, destroying the centre of the building. In 1801-03 a large part of the sculpture that remained was removed, with Turkish permission, by the British nobleman Thomas Bruce, Lord Elgin, and sold in 1816 to the British Museum in London. Other sculptures from the Parthenon are now in the Louvre Museum in Paris, in Copenhagen, and elsewhere, but many are still in Athens.

but bulge slightly toward their middles in entasis. Thus the whole building was treated with the subtlety and delicacy of the marble sculptures that filled its metopes and pediment. The attitude of Callicrates and Ictinus toward religious architecture ceased to be that of the superstitious priest-architect held subject to unvaryingly precise (and often hypnotically elaborate) repetition of prescribed forms and became instead that of the artist rationalist—adjusting, refining, and simplifying forms to make them quietly effective and satisfying to the eye.

HELLENISTIC PERIOD

In the 5th century BCE, the age of Pericles, Greece was still an assortment of independent city-states, many of them democracies. In 338 BCE Philip II of Macedon forced them all together into a single empire. Between 334 and 323 his son, Alexander the Great, conquered Egypt, Mesopotamia, Iran, and parts of India, transforming the whole into the most powerful state in the civilized world. Greek architecture suddenly became that of this rich, powerful Hellenic empire and was forced to break out of the fixed, small-scale vocabulary of forms that had been satisfactory for the Periclean temple. The orders were retained and a new one added, the Corinthian, a variation of the Ionic with realistic leaves of the acanthus plant on its capital. Construction was still in stone blocks—preferably marble—following the system of the column-post and entablature-lintel. But now this simple system was extended and multiplied to make monumental cities with colonnaded avenues and squares, palaces and public meeting halls, libraries and tombs. A series of great Hellenistic metropolises grew up, Alexandria in Egypt in particular (today completely buried underneath the modern city). At the royal city of Pergamum, which was built during the 3rd and 2nd centuries BCE, one can see even today a series of colonnaded

Ruins of a Roman amphitheatre in the ancient city of Pergamum, which is located in present-day Turkey. Roman rule followed Greek rule of the site, and remains of both cultures can still be viewed today.

plazas stepping up a concave hillside, a single huge composition of architectural forms that are expressive of Hellenistic wealth and political power.

This was no longer an architecture of detail and refinement but one of massive (if simple) construction and political show. The vocabulary of the Periclean temple was no longer appropriate, and the Roman Empire that succeeded the Hellenistic adopted another, revolutionary solution.

ROMAN AND EARLY CHRISTIAN ARCHITECTURE

The Roman Empire, founded by Augustus Caesar in 27 BCE and lasting in Western Europe for 500 years, reorganized world politics and economics. Almost the entirety of the civilized world became

as a villa the size of a small city for himself at Tivoli. Later Caracalla (211–217) and Diocletian (284–305) erected two mammoth baths that bear their names, and Maxentius (306–312) built a huge vaulted basilica, now called the Basilica of Constantine.

The Baths of Caracalla have long been accepted as a summation of Roman culture and engineering. It is a vast building, 360 by 702 feet (110 by 214 metres), set in 50 acres (20 hectares) of gardens. It was one of a dozen establishments of similar size in ancient Rome devoted to recreation and bathing. There were a 60- by 120-foot (18- by 36-metre) swimming pool, hot and cold baths (each not much smaller than the pool), gymnasia, a library, and game rooms. These rooms were of various geometric shapes. The walls were thick, with recesses, corridors, and staircases cut into them. The building was entirely constructed of concrete with barrel, groined, and domical vaults spanning as far as 60 feet (18 metres) in many places. Inside, all the walls were covered with thin slabs of coloured marble or with painted stucco. The decorative forms of this coating, strangely enough, were derived from Greek architecture as though the Romans could build but could not ornament. Therefore, what is Roman about the Baths of Caracalla and the other great constructions of the Romans is merely the skeleton.

The Baths of Caracalla in Rome were completed in 217 CE by Alexander Severus. There were three large vaulted bath chambers and a central great hall, with courts and auxiliary rooms, surrounded by a garden for exercise and games. Caracalla is the largest surviving great Roman bath.

The rebuilding of Rome set a pattern copied all over the empire. Nearby, the ruins of Ostia, Rome's port (principally constructed in the 2nd and 3rd centuries CE), reflect that model. Farther away it reappears at Trier in northwestern Germany, at Autun in central France, at Antioch in Syria, and at Timgad and Leptis Magna in North Africa. When political disintegration and barbarian invasions disrupted the western part of the Roman Empire in the 4th century CE, new cities were founded and built in concrete during short construction campaigns: Ravenna, the capital of the Western Empire from 492–539, and Constantinople in Turkey, where the seat of the empire was moved by Constantine in 330 and which continued thereafter to be the capital of the Eastern, or Byzantine, Empire.

CHRISTIAN ROME

One important thing had changed by the time of the founding of Ravenna and Constantinople; after 313 this was the Christian Roman Empire. The principal challenge to the imperial architects was now the construction of churches. These churches were large vaulted enclosures of interior space, unlike the temples of the Greeks and the pagan Romans that were mere statue-chambers set in open precincts. The earliest imperial churches in Rome, like the first church of St. Peter's erected by Constantine from 333, were vast barns with wooden roofs supported on lines of columns. They resembled basilicas, which had carried on the Hellenistic style of columnar architecture. Roman concrete vaulted construction was used in certain cases, for example, in the tomb church in Rome of Constantine's daughter, Santa Costanza, of about 350. In the church of San Vitale in Ravenna, erected in 526–547, this was expanded to the scale of a middle-sized church. Here a domed octagon 60 feet (18 metres) across is surrounded by a corridor, or aisle, and balcony 30 feet (9 metres) deep. On each side a semicircular projection from the central space pushes outward to blend these spaces together.

In the 5th century, as local schools formed, the unity of Christian architecture with that of the empire ceased to exist. In Italy, although basilicas of the Classical type continued to be built, they assimilated Eastern influences. North Africa modified the basilica plan only by multiplying the number of side aisles (Damous-el-Karita in Carthage has eight) or by adding apses.

The ecclesiastical architecture of the East is more varied, partly as a result of differences in the liturgies. In Syria, Israel, and Jordan a particularly large number of 5th-, 6th-, and 7th-century churches are preserved. The triple influence of the Greek countries, Constantinople, and the imperial sanctuaries of the Holy Land resulted in many plans, whereas the materials and construction methods remained in the tradition of the region.

The ties between the Latin West and the Greek East, particularly strong in the 4th and 5th centuries, relaxed in the 6th. Beginning with the reign of Justinian, a true Byzantine architecture developed from the new capital. In the western Mediterranean, the end of the ancient world and of early Christian architecture came with the fall of the Roman Empire in 476.

CHAPTER TWO

BYZANTINE ARCHITECTURE

The symbolic religious buildings of Egypt, Mesopotamia, India, Japan, and Greece stood apart from the surrounding cities and stated a religious belief in every detail. The Byzantine church, however, was buried in the new masonry city, another domical block like the baths and basilicas nearby. But symbolic expression found a new and powerful medium in the illusionistic decoration of the vast interior church spaces. The interiors of the Baths of Caracalla had been decorated with fragments of Greek architecture, and the walls of Nero's Domus Aurea had been painted in fantastic stage architecture and landscapes. Now the interior of the Byzantine church was covered with glass mosaic pieces. These depicted Biblical scenes and images of saints set against a continuous gold background. The mosaics at Hagia Sophia have been plastered over, but an impression of the original effect survives in the smaller, later churches at Daphni and

Gold mosaics adorn the interior of the San Marco Basilica, giving it the nickname the Church of Gold. Viewed in certain lights, the colours of the mosaics and the marble and glass floor glow.

Hosios Loukas and, especially, San Marco in Venice, begun in 1063. Here the walls of the space are made to disappear in a glow of mystical light, and the worshipper seems to be carried up into the court of Heaven with Christ and all the saints.

THE EARLY BYZANTINE PERIOD (330-726)

When Constantine began to build his new capital on the Bosporus, a mass of artisans was assembled for the purpose. The majority of them were drawn from Rome, so that, at first, official art was early Christian in style and was, in fact, virtually Roman art: the Classical basilica was adopted as the usual type of Christian church; portrait statues of emperors were set up as in pagan times, and sarcophagi were elaborately sculptured; floor mosaics of Classical character were widely used; and works in ivory and metal retained a basically Roman character. Change was in the air, however, even before the capital had been moved from Rome. In architecture the post-and-lintel style in stone, which had been taken over from the Greeks, was already giving place to an architecture of arches, vaults, and domes in brick, whereas sculptural ornament was becoming more formal and less naturalistic. These changes were accelerated at Constantinople partly because of the proximity of the city to Asia Minor and Syria, both fertile centres of new artistic ideas that had developed independently of Rome. Indeed, church architecture in those areas progressed considerably between the 4th and the 6th centuries, while in the visual arts a style that favoured formality and expression rather than the idealized naturalism of Classical art had begun to find approval at an early date.

Constantine's new capital was carefully laid out and boasted an important series of secular buildings—walls, hippodrome, forums, public buildings, arcaded streets, and an imperial palace—all of great magnificence. The religious structures he set up were of two principal types: longitudinal basilicas and centralized churches. The former, usually with three aisles, were intended for congregational worship; the latter, which were circular, square, or even octagonal, were for burial or commemorative usage. Both types were to be found over a very wide area, though there were, of course, numerous local variations. It was through a subtle combination of the two types that the characteristic church of the Byzantine Empire emerged, thanks to some experiments made in the eastern Mediterranean area in the 5th century. The progress cannot be followed exactly because so much has been destroyed, but

The domed roof and brick arches typical of Byzantine churches can be seen in the 12th-century Panagia Kosmosoteira in Evros, Greece, pictured here.

the earliest surviving church in Constantinople, St. John of Studium (Mosque of Imrahor), shows that this process had already gone quite far by the year it was built, 463. It is a basilica in that it has an eastern apse and three aisles, but in plan it approaches a centralized building, for it is nearly square, in contrast to the long basilicas in vogue in Rome. A similar change characterizes the sculptures that adorn its facade, for they are in low relief, in contrast with typical Roman high-relief sculpture, and the motifs are treated formally, as pieces of pattern, rather than as depictions of natural forms.

The process of development that began in such examples had greatly advanced by the end of the century, as remains discovered in the 1960s of the church of St. Polyeuktos show. The church was founded by the princess Juliana Anicia (granddaughter of Valentinian III), whose name is known from an illuminated manuscript dated 512. The change was advanced still further some 30 years later, thanks to the patronage of the emperor Justinian, one of the greatest builders of all time. He was responsible for four major churches in Constantinople: Saints Sergius and Bacchus, a centralized building; the church of St. Eirene (Irene), a basilica roofed by two domes in echelon (i.e., parallel-stepped arrangement); the church of the Holy Apostles, which was cruciform, with a dome at the crossing and another on each of the arms of the cross; and, finally, the great cathedral of Hagia Sophia, where the ideas of longitudinal basilica and centralized building were combined in a wholly original manner. The distinctive feature of all these structures was the form of roof, the dome. In Saints Sergius and Bacchus it stood on an octagonal base, so that no great problems were involved in

THE PENDENTIVE AND SQUINCH

A pendentive is a triangular segment of a spherical surface, filling in the upper corners of a room, in order to form, at the top, a circular support for a dome. The challenge of supporting a dome over an enclosed square or polygonal space assumed growing importance to the Roman builders of the late empire. It remained for Byzantine architects, however, to recognize the possibilities of the pendentive and fully develop it. One of the earliest examples of the use of the pendentive is also one of the largest—that of Hagia Sophia (completed 537 CE) at Istanbul.

Pendentives are common in the Romanesque domed churches of the Aquitaine in France, as in Saint-Front at Perigueux (begun 1120) and the cathedral of Saint-Pierre at Angoulême (1105–28), but they occur only occasionally in Italian churches. During the Renaissance and the Baroque, the preference for domed churches, especially in Roman Catholic Europe and Latin America, gave great importance to the pendentive. As a result of Byzantine influence, pendentives are frequently used in Islamic architecture. They are often decorated with stalactite work or sometimes, as in Iran, with delicate ribbing.

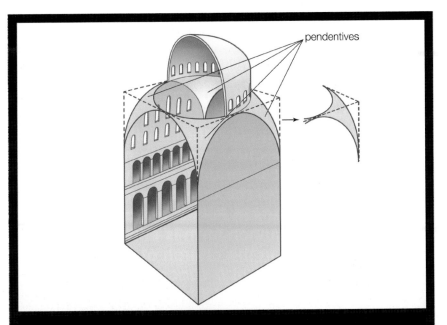

pendentives

A dome of the Hagia Sophia shows pendentive construction. The Hagia Sophia has one of the earliest and largest examples of the pendentive.

A vaulting form in which the curve of the pendentive and dome is continuous, without a break, is known as a pendentive dome.

A squinch is any of several devices by which a square or polygonal room has its upper corners filled in to form a support for a dome: by corbelling out the courses of masonry, each course projecting slightly beyond the one below; by building one or more arches diagonally across the corner; by building in the corner a niche with a half dome at its head; or by filling the corner

(continued on the next page)

(continued from the previous page)

with a little conical vault that has an arch on its outer diagonal face and its apex in the corner.

The arched squinch that is often used in Byzantine architecture seems to have been developed, almost simultaneously, by the Roman builders of the late imperial period and the Sasanians in Persia. In Italy the Romanesque squinch form is either the conical type as in the church of Sant' Ambrogio at Milan or a succession of arched rings as in the 13th-century central tower of the abbey church at Chiaravalle. More complex forms with niches and colonnettes are characteristic of the French Romanesque of Auvergny, as in the cathedral of Le Puy-en-Velay (late 11th and early 12th centuries); churches of southwestern France, such as Saint-Hilaire at Poitiers, use conical squinches of the Italian type.

Islamic architecture, borrowing from the Sasanian precedent, makes great use of squinch forms. The stalactite work, which is so marked a feature of later Islamic architecture, is, in essence, merely a decorative development of a combination of niche squinch forms. In Gothic architecture squinch arches are frequently used on the insides of square towers to support octagonal spires.

converting the angular ground plan to a circle on which the dome could rest. But in the others the dome stands above a square, and the transition from the one to the other was complicated. Two separate processes of doing this had evolved: the squinch, a niche or arch in the corner of the square, which transformed it into an octagon, over which the dome could be placed without great difficulty; and the pendentive, a spherical triangle fitted into the corners of the square, its vertical sides corresponding to the curves of the arches supporting the dome and its upper side corresponding to the circular base of the drum.

Though Justinian's domed basilicas are the models from which Byzantine architecture developed, Hagia Sophia remained unique, and no attempt was thereafter made by Byzantine builders to emulate it. In plan it is almost square, but looked at from within, it appears to be rectangular, for there is a great semidome at east and west above that prolongs the effect of the roof, while on the ground there are three aisles, separated by columns with galleries above. At either end, however, great piers rise up through the galleries to support the dome. Above the galleries are curtain walls (non-load-bearing exterior walls) at either side, pierced by windows, and there are more windows at the base of the dome. The columns are of finest marble, selected for their colour and variety, while the lower parts of the walls are covered with marble slabs. Like the elaborately carved cornices and capitals, these survive, but the rest of the original decoration, including most of the mosaics that adorned the upper parts of the walls and the roof, has perished. They were all described in the most glowing terms by early writers. But enough does survive to warrant the inclusion of Hagia Sophia in the list of the world's greatest buildings. It was built as the result of the destruction in a riot of its predecessor, the basilica begun by Constantine, and the work of rebuilding was completed in the amazingly short period of five years, 10 months, and four

days, under the direction of two architects from Asia Minor, Anthemius of Tralles and Isidorus of Miletus, in the year 537.

The Hagia Sophia, still standing in what is now Istanbul, Turkey, remains one of the foremost Byzantine structures. Its minarets, added in the 15th century after the church had been repurposed as a mosque, can also be seen here.

HAGIA SOPHIA

The Hagia Sophia is a cathedral that was built in Constantinople (now Istanbul, Turkey) in the 6th century CE (532–537) under the direction of the Byzantine emperor Justinian I. By general consensus, it is the most important Byzantine structure and one of the world's great monuments.

The Hagia Sophia combines a longitudinal basilica and a centralized building in a wholly original manner, with a huge 105-foot (32-metre) main dome supported on pendentives and two semidomes, one on either side of the longitudinal axis. In plan the building is almost square. There are three aisles separated by columns with galleries above and great marble piers rising up to support the dome. The walls above the galleries and the base of the dome are pierced by windows, which in the glare of daylight obscure the supports and give the impression that the canopy floats on air.

The Hagia Sophia was built in the remarkably short time of about six years. Unusual for the period in which it was built, the names of the building's architects—Anthemius of Tralles and Isidorus of Miletus—are well known, as is their familiarity with mechanics and mathematics.

The original church on the site of the Hagia Sophia is said to have been built by Constantine I in 325 on the foundations of a pagan temple. It was rebuilt after a fire in 404 (upon the second banishment of St. John Chrysostom, then patriarch of Constantinople) and enlarged by the Roman emperor Constans I. The restored building was rededicated in 415 by Theodosius II. The church was burned again in the Nika insurrection of January 532, a circumstance that gave Justinian I an opportunity to envision a splendid replacement.

The structure now standing is essentially the 6th-century edifice, although an earthquake caused a partial collapse of the dome in 558 (restored 562) and there were two further partial collapses, after which it was rebuilt to a smaller scale and the whole church reinforced from the outside. It was restored again in the mid-14th century. For more than a millennium it was the Cathedral of the Ecumenical Patriarchate of Constantinople. It was looted in 1204 by the Venetians and the Crusaders on the Fourth Crusade. After the Turkish conquest of Constantinople in 1453, Mehmed II had it repurposed as a mosque, with the addition

(continued on the next page)

(continued from the previous page)

of minarets (on the exterior, towers used for the summons to prayer), a great chandelier, a *mihrab* (niche indicating the direction of Mecca), a *minbar* (pulpit), and disks bearing Islamic calligraphy. Kemal Atatürk secularized the building in 1934, and in 1935 it was made into a museum. Art historians consider the building's beautiful mosaics to be the main source of knowledge about the state of mosaic art in the time shortly after the end of the Iconoclastic Controversy in the 8th and 9th centuries. The Hagia Sophia is a component of a UNESCO World Heritage site called the Historic Areas of Istanbul (designated 1985), which includes that city's other major historic buildings and locations.

From the little known it would seem that similar changes were taking place in secular architecture. The walls of the city, which still in greater part survive, were set up under Theodosius II (408–50) early in the 5th century, and already the method of construction (where a number of courses of brick alternate with those of stone) and the forms of vaulting used to support the floors in the numerous towers show several innovations. The walls themselves, a triple line of defense, with 192 towers at alternate intervals in the inner and middle wall, were far in advance of anything erected previously; they were, indeed, so well-conceived that they served to protect the city against every assault until the Turks, supported by cannon, attacked with vastly superior odds in 1453. Also distinctive were the underground cisterns, of which more than 30 are known in Constantinople today. They all took on the same character, with strong outer walls and roofs of small domes supported on tall columns. Some are of great size, some comparatively small. In some, like the great cistern near Hagia Sophia called by the Turks the Yerebatan (Underground) Palace, old material was reused; in others, like the even more impressive Binbirdirek (Thousand and One Columns) cistern, new columns of unusually tall and slender proportions and new capitals of cubic form were designed specially. These cisterns assured an adequate supply of water even when the aqueducts that fed the city were cut by an attacking enemy. Many of them were still in use at the end of the 19th century. Contemporary texts show that the houses were often large and elaborate and had at least two stories, while the imperial palace was built on enormous terraces of masonry on the slopes bordering the upper shores of the Sea of Marmara. The palace was founded by Constantine, but practically every subsequent emperor added to it, and it eventually became a vast conglomeration of buildings extending over more than 100 acres (40 hectares). Many of the buildings were of a very original character, if the descriptions that survive are to be believed; unfortunately, nearly all have been destroyed in the course of time.

THE ICONOCLASTIC AGE (726-843)

A common theme in the history of Byzantium of this period is the attempt to ban the veneration of icons (the representation of saintly or divine personages). This Iconoclastic Controversy raged for a century, from the time Iconoclasm became an imperial policy under Leo III in 730 until icon veneration was officially proclaimed as Orthodox belief in 843. In spite of this controversy, and the reduced prosperity of the state during this period, churches continued to be built, including the church of the Assumption at Nicaea (now Iznik, Turkey) and Ayía Sofía at Thessalonica (Thessaloníki). The emperors were not necessarily opposed to all building and art, however. It is known from texts that Theophilus (829–842) was responsible for numerous additions to the Great Palace.

THE MIDDLE BYZANTINE PERIOD (843–1204)

The most understanding of the emperors in the years immediately succeeding Iconoclasm was Basil I (867–886). Like many of his predecessors, he built in the area of the Great Palace, his most

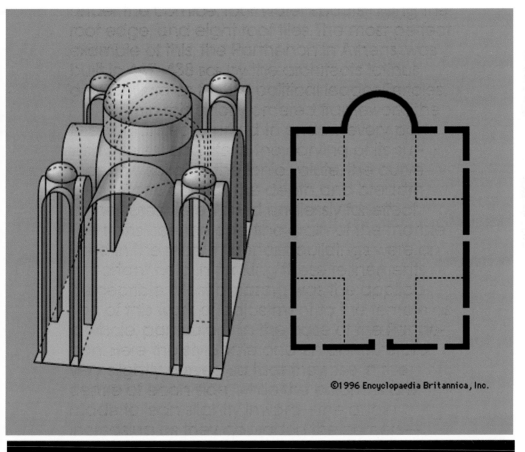

©1996 Encyclopaedia Britannica, Inc.

(Left) Perspective drawing of a quincunx, or five-domed, church, a church type of the second Golden Age based on the domed cross element; *(right)* plan of church, showing cross-in-square design.

interesting contributions being two churches, the New Church and the church of the Theotokos of the Pharos. These set a fashion in church building and decoration that was to exercise an influence for many centuries. Neither survives, but something is known of them from written descriptions; it would seem that both were typical of what was to be the mid-Byzantine style. Broadly speaking, the churches of this age conform to a single type, usually termed the cross-in-square. It is made up of three aisles, each one terminating in an apsidal chapel at the east, with a transverse nave at the west. Invariably, there was a dome over the central aisle, supported on four columns, with four vaults radiating from it to roof the central aisle to the west, the sanctuary to the east, and the central portions of the side aisles to the north and south. These vaults rose above the roofs of the other portions of the building, so that the church was cruciform at roof level. Excluding the transverse nave, the churches were usually almost as broad as they were long, making the basic plan virtually a square. Occasionally, additional columns were used to extend the nave westward, producing a type known as the domed basilica; sometimes the walls separating the eastern ends of the side aisles from the central presbytery were extended westward as substitutes for the two eastern columns upholding the dome, but the essentials of the plan were always retained. Subsidiary domes were sometimes added, either in place of the vaults on the arms of the cross, producing a true five-domed type such as St. Mark's Cathedral at Venice, or placed above the eastern and western extremities of the side aisles. These domes were usually comparatively small and were set on drums, which tended to become narrower and taller with the progress of time. The eastern extremities of the side aisles formed chapels, which played an important part in the liturgy. Both the chapels and the main sanctuary were separated from the body of the church by a screen, which also became taller and heavier until it developed into the massive iconostasis that constitutes such a characteristic feature of Orthodox churches today. As in earlier periods, the lower portions of the walls were, in the richer churches, covered with marble slabs; and there were elaborately carved cornices and capitals, though ornament was always rather formal and in low relief. The main church at the monastery of St. Luke near Delphi, in Greece (*c.* 1050), is the most complete surviving example of the type.

THE LATE BYZANTINE PERIOD (1204–1453)

Quite a number of buildings from the late Byzantine period survive in Istanbul,

CHAPTER THREE

ARCHITECTURE IN THE MIDDLE AGES: THE CHRISTIAN WEST

For seven centuries, from 300 to 1000, Europe was a shambles of crude wooden houses and churches. This was in sharp contrast to the continuation of Roman building techniques in the Byzantine and Islamic empires in the East. There had been only one short break in these Dark Ages: the reign of Charlemagne (768–814) was marked by the erection of his palace and palace chapel (792–805) at Aachen (now in Germany), which is a copy of San Vitale in Ravenna. Shortly after 1000, however, a miraculous transformation occurred. Large masonry churches were simultaneously begun all over Europe. The 11th-century monk Raoul Glaber wrote that it was as if the continent was putting on "a white mantle of churches." This was religious architecture built by anonymous architects according to symbolic prescriptions.

ROMANESQUE

In the Middle Ages the population of Europe had diminished by half since Roman times. Communication and transport, either by land or by sea, might be difficult or hazardous, and this tended naturally to divide the country into neighbourhoods. Under these conditions, a great monastery, like a city, could serve a considerable surrounding area as an administrative, intellectual, and spiritual centre and as a workshop, granary, and refuge. With increasing prosperity the monastic building complexes were progressively better organized, better built, and more impressive. Showing the way for cathedral and domestic architecture, the great patrons of the age were the abbots, though not to the exclusion of the bishops and magnates.

ROMAN FOUNDATIONS

The Romans had not solved the problem of the fireproof basilican church—a problem that became pressing with the frequent conflagrations in timber-built towns and, not less, the incendiarism that was a lamentable consequence of endemic local wars and the incursions of organized marauders. By 1000 CE the monastic builders had begun to solve this problem by vaulting. Moreover, they had improved upon the Roman attempts at systematic plans for the monasteries themselves, which might accommodate 1,000 persons—monks, brethren, craftsmen, servants, slaves, and guests—with provision for their multiple activities and also suitable storage facilities.

The solution, well exemplified in the plan of 820 for the monastery at St. Gall, was a quadrangular court, or cloister, provided with arcaded walks, or "alleys," and placed beside the nave of the church. Typically, the east walk had an entrance into the church near the sanctuary; and the members of the community, entering processionally, would turn into their choir enclosure in the nave, while the celebrants would occupy their posts in the sanctuary. Important rooms bordered the east walk: the chapter house, where the community met as a corporation; the parlour, where speaking was allowed for the transaction of business; and the camera, or workroom. The walk parallel to the church gave access to the calefactory (in early times often the only heated room) for fellowship, the refectory, the pantries, and the kitchens. The cellars stretched along the west walk between the kitchens and a porter's lodge adjoining the church. The door at the porter's lodge was the principal entrance to the cloister. The scriptorium and library were typically in the walk beside the church; the dormitory was usually located directly above the buildings of the east walk.

CLOISTER

A cloister is a quadrilateral enclosure surrounded by covered walkways and usually
attached to a monastic or cathedral church
and sometimes to a college. The term used
in a narrow sense also applies to the walkways or alleys themselves (the central area
being the cloister garth), in a general sense
to the houses of religious orders, and in a
generic sense to places of retreat for religious purposes.

(continued on the next page)

The covered walkway of a monastery, such as the one seen here,
is often referred to as a cloister. The term more broadly includes the
quadrilateral that is enclosed by such walkways.

(continued from the previous page)

A cloister is usually the area in a monastery around which the principal buildings are ranged, affording a means of communication between the buildings. In developed medieval practice, cloisters usually followed either a Benedictine or a Cistercian arrangement. In the Benedictine form, the church was located on one side of the cloister, with the refectory occupying the opposite side, so that the worshippers might be removed from kitchen noises and smells. The chapter house was placed on the eastern side, with other apartments adjacent to it and the dormitory usually occupying the entire upper story. On the western side, the cellarer's lodgings were generally located, near storehouses that held the community's provisions.

In Cistercian monasteries the western side of the cloister was usually occupied by the two-story *domus conversorum*, or lodgings of the lay brothers, with their day rooms and workshops situated beneath the dormitory. The buildings generally stood on the south of the church to get as much sunshine as possible.

The cloister of a religious house was the centre of activity for its inhabitants. There the younger members were educated and the elders studied. The west walk was traditionally, if unofficially, the place of educational instruction. The other walkways, especially the one next to the church, were devoted to the studies of the elder monks, and for this purpose small studies (known as carols, or carrels) were often built into the recesses of the windows. The cloister also served for exercise and general recreation, particularly in bad weather, and its central area and walkways were the customary places of burial.

Larger monastic establishments commonly had more than one cloister; there was usually a second connected with the infirmary (e.g., at Westminster Abbey and Canterbury) and sometimes one giving access to the kitchen and other domestic offices. Cloisters were also attached to colleges of secular canons, as at the cathedrals of Lincoln, Salisbury, and Wells; and the colleges of Eton and Winchester, as well as New College and Magdalen College at Oxford, also have cloisters.

The earliest cloisters consisted of open arcades, usually with sloping wooden roofs. This form of the cloister was generally superseded in England by a range of windows, usually unglazed but sometimes, as at Gloucester, provided with glass, lighting a vaulted ambulatory. In southern climates, the open-arcaded

(continued on the next page)

(continued from the previous page)

cloister remained standard; of this type are the cloisters of Saint-Trophîme at Arles in southern France, Santo Domingo de Silos in Spain, and the Belém Monastery near Lisbon, all of which are famous for their sculptural decoration.

The open cloister attained its fullest development in Italy, however. A fine example, damaged beyond full repair during World War II, was the Campo Santo at Pisa, consisting of four ambulatories as wide and lofty as the nave of a church, with inner walls covered with early Renaissance frescoes. An especially fine example of the Renaissance cloister is provided by Donato Bramante's design for the two-story open arcade at Santa Maria della Pace in Rome.

This plan was very flexible, for in a large monastery there would be several cloisters or courts with suitable independent arrangements for archives, administration, guests, wayfarers, servants, artisans, shops, and folds; special quarters were provided by such courts for retired or sick monks and for novices. Special chapels were provided, where necessary, in these subsidiary parts of the establishment.

The several cloisters or courts of a large monastery carried on the tradition established by the greater Germanic households of the pagan time; they too were composed of "proliferating quadrangles." The basic unit, as has been learned from excavation, was a wide, framed, compartmented longhouse with a steep, thatched roof. By Charlemagne's time longhouses of this type were sometimes adapted as churches.

CHURCHES

Though Rome could no longer present fresh models for universal emulation or exercise unifying control, its architectural monuments were still numerous in many regions and could not be ignored. A new period of architecture commenced, called Romanesque today because it was the reproduction of Roman vaulted style. The methods of construction were the same, although often very crudely carried out, but great originality was shown in interior spatial planning and in exterior massing and decoration. A new type of church evolved that is excellently represented in St. Sernin at Toulouse, built from about 1080 to 1120. The plan is cross-shaped instead of centralized as at Hagia Sophia. The longest of its four arms extends westward and is the nave. It is crossed by shorter

The nave of the church of St. Sernin in Toulouse is the longest arm of the cross-shaped structure. The heavy vaults are an example of Roman influence.

transepts and is balanced by a short chevet, or head, where the altar is set in front of a semicircular end-wall roofed with a half-dome. Each arm has an aisle on either side below a high balcony, or triforium. These arms are vaulted with simple half-cylindrical barrel vaults and are narrow so that the intersection, or crossing, is less important for the tiny dome inside than for the tall tower built in tiers above it on the exterior. In the chevet the aisles are carried around the curved end as an ambulatory from which open individual semicircular chapels.

Romanesque churches of this type are in France and northern Spain and Italy and have been called pilgrimage churches because they stand along the route of pilgrimage roads leading to San Juan Campostella. Relics were displayed for veneration in the chapels around the chevet, and sleeping space for pilgrims was provided in the triforium.

Other similar Romanesque church types developed all over Europe. Along the Rhine River large churches were built with narrow, vaulted naves, no transepts, and groups of tall towers at both ends. In northern France the Norman Romanesque evolved with skillful vaulting and pairs of tall towers at the west facades. This style was carried to England by William the Conqueror after 1066 and produced the Anglo-Norman Romanesque of Durham and Ely cathedrals. The Romanesque's most striking manifestation was probably in Italy, among the ruins of the ancient Roman Empire and near the continuing Byzantine culture. Here trading cities were experiencing new prosperity. The Venetians, beginning in 1063, built San Marco with five domes, an elaborate imitation of Byzantine architecture. In Pisa, beginning in 1053, a complex of structures was built—a cathedral, bell tower, baptistery, and monumental cemetery—of sparkling coloured marbles covered with carved decoration, in part Roman, in part fantastic and barbarian.

FORTIFICATIONS

While such religious architecture dominated the Middle Ages, there were also important architectural expressions of secular power.

The Normans were among the first in Europe to build elaborate fortifications and castles. These were built to overwhelm the populace, and they served a variety of functions, including royal residences, treasury houses, prisons, administrative centres, and bases from which the surrounding countryside could be controlled. One such construction, the White Tower (begun *c.* 1078) at the Tower of London, was built as much to express William I the Conqueror's wealth and authority as to secure his safety and that of the court. Some of the most sophisticated of all castles were those erected in southern Italy in the 1230s and '40s by the Holy Roman emperor, Frederick II of Hohenstaufen; of particular note is the octagonal Castel del Monte in Andria, in the Puglia region. These structures influenced the building of the circular castle palace of Bellver (1309–14) in Palma, as well as Welsh castles from the late 13th century such as Harlech Castle, which was characterized by concentric forms. Like the earlier commissions of Frederick II, these structures celebrated pure geometry through symmetrical patterns. Great castles such as Villandraut, built by the first French pope at Avignon and perhaps inspired by the Welsh model, were also constructed in France in the 13th through 15th centuries. The 14th-century fortress palace of Marienburg (now Malbork, Poland), near Danzig (now Gdansk, Poland), is among the most impressive structures of its kind.

Related to these strongholds, the construction of fortified cities also characterized the period. Beginning in the late 11th century in Spain, polygonal walls were built to encompass the ancient city of Ávila; this represented the impulse, frequent during the period, for a ruling or royal family to overcome revolt from barons through architectural means. By the 13th and 14th centuries in France, walled cities such as Carcassonne and Aigues-Mortes were developed. Laid out in a grid plan, Aigues-Mortes is one of the largest surviving fortified towns of the Middle Ages. Other forms of secular architecture also emerged during the period: Flanders, Belgium, and Italy were notable for their monumental town halls, cloth halls, and guild halls, especially as seen in Antwerp, Arras, Brussels, Bruges, Ypres, Florence, and Siena.

GOTHIC

The prosperity and the building campaigns of the Romanesque period were slight, however, in comparison to the vast development of economic and building power of the Gothic period, which began in the late 12th century. In France, between 1140 and 1200, a new and

more efficient type of masonry vaulted construction was invented. The Roman vault was
a consistent mass of concrete that had been
poured over a heavy wooden mold and left
to harden. The new Gothic vault consisted of
a network of separate stone arches, or ribs,
spanning the space, between which were
laid a thin webbing of small stones. This kind
of vault was lighter and its thrusts were more
clearly defined, since they passed down the
ribs. This meant that the walls of the building
supporting the vaults could be made thinner
and opened with large windows. Furthermore,
beginning in 1194 with the construction of
Chartres Cathedral, the weight of these vaults
was supported on flying buttresses, light structures of stone piers and arches standing
outside the mass of the building itself.

The plan of a Gothic church resembled that of the Romanesque but was more
unified because the arms were shorter, the
spaces broader, and the walls between the
parts were made thinner or entirely removed.
Gothic interior spaces, however, did not look
at all the same. The efficient vaulting system
enabled these spaces to be much taller and
to be entirely surrounded with windows that
were filled with stained glass depicting Biblical
scenes and saints. These figures, in deep reds
and blues, seem to float above the worshipper
like the figures depicted in Byzantine mosaics,
but they glowed as daylight beamed through.

CHARTRES CATHEDRAL

Also called the Cathedral of Notre-Dame, Chartres is a Gothic cathedral named for the town in which it was built in northwestern France. Generally ranked as one of the three chief examples of Gothic French architecture (along with the Amiens and Reims cathedrals), it is noted not only for its architectural innovations but also for its numerous sculptures and its much-celebrated stained glass. The cathedral's association with the Virgin Mary (the supposed veil of the Virgin is kept in the cathedral treasury) made it a pilgrim destination in the Middle Ages.

The oldest parts of the cathedral are its crypt and the west portal, or Royal Portal, which are remnants of a Romanesque church that was mostly destroyed by fire in 1194. The present cathedral was constructed on the foundations of the earlier church and consecrated in 1260. It is built of limestone and stands some 112 feet (34 metres) high and is 427 feet (130 metres) long. In many ways, the cathedral's design resembles those of its contemporaries, especially Laon Cathedral, but it displays innovations with its tall arcades, unusually narrow triforium,

Flying buttresses, such as the ones seen on the right-hand side of this image of the Chartres Cathedral, extend ("fly") from the upper part of a wall to a pier some distance away and carry the thrust of a roof or vault.

and huge clerestory—the massive weight of which required using flying buttresses in an unprecedented manner.

The cathedral contains an immense amount of sculpture, particularly figure sculpture, ranging from large column statues to miniatures. As the purpose of the sculptures was to preach and instruct, they

(continued on the next page)

(continued from the previous page)

mainly depict scenes and figures from the Old and New Testaments.

Chartres Cathedral is probably best-known for its 176 stained-glass windows. Like the sculpture, the stained glass was intended to be educational. The five windows of the choir hemicycle (a semicircular arrangement) relate in various ways to the Virgin Mary. The rose window in the north transept portrays figures from the Old Testament. The south transept, which is representative of the New Testament, has a rose window depicting the Apocalypse.

Several alterations have been made to the cathedral. The northwest tower's distinctive spire, for example, was added in the early 1500s. Chartres emerged with relatively little damage from the political and religious upheavals of the 16th century and sustained less damage than most cathedrals during the French Revolution (1787–99). After a fire damaged the roof in 1836, a series of restorations were carried out during the 19th century. In 1979 Chartres Cathedral was designated a UNESCO World Heritage site. During the late 20th century, preservation efforts concentrated on protecting the cathedral's stained glass from air pollution damage.

To hold these great expanses of glass in place, thin stone ribs of tracery in decorative forms were built across the windows.

Externally the Gothic church was more complex and expressive than the Romanesque. Tall towers with tiers of openings and slender stone spires marked at least the facade and crossing, and usually were intended at the transept ends as well. Along the sides flying buttresses stood out from the wall and bore pinnacles and tracery as well as carved figures and fantastic rainspouts called gargoyles. At the doors at the end of the nave, and sometimes also at those at the ends of the transepts, were elaborate symbolic sculptural compositions of Biblical scenes and saints. Above would sometimes be a huge round stained-glass rose window. The Gothic style was used not only in the construction of churches but, like the Roman vaulted style, was a building technique and permitted a whole city-full of masonry vaulted forms to be created.

Although Europe was as prosperous as it had been under the

The concentric city walls of Harlech Castle in Wales, seen in this aerial photograph, represent an important advance in defense and a significant achievement of Gothic architecture.

Romans, it was disturbed by continual wars between the separate city-states. Thus the finest achievements of the Gothic builders were the mighty rings of city walls, like those at Carcassonne in France, or castles, like Harlech Castle in England. Inside these were expansive rib-vaulted rooms and chapels. In the free-trading cities of France, the Netherlands, and northern Germany, there arose large town halls, like the Cloth Hall (about 1250–1300) at Ypres (now in Belgium). There were also palaces such as that at Nuremberg, with its wooden beamed ceiling. Rich merchants built expensive houses with traceried windows and carved fireplaces, as Jacques Coeur did in Bourges, France, in 1443–51.

THE END OF GOTHIC

The change from late Gothic to Renaissance was superficially far less cataclysmic than the change from Romanesque to Gothic. In the figurative arts, it was not the great shift from symbolism to realistic representation but a change from one sort of realism to another.

Architecturally, as well, the initial changes involved decorative material. For this reason, the early stages of Renaissance art outside Italy are hard to disentangle from late Gothic. Monuments like the huge Franche-Comté chantry chapel at Brou (1513–32) may have intermittent Italian motifs, but the general effect intended was not very different from that of Henry VII's Chapel at Westminster. The Shrine of St. Sebaldus at Nuremberg (1508–19) has the general shape of a Gothic tomb with canopy, although much of the detail is Italianate. In fact, for artists between about 1500 and 1530 throughout Europe, the "Italian Renaissance" meant the *enjolivement*, or embellishment of an already rich decorative repertoire with shapes, motifs, and figures adapted from another canon of taste. The history of the northern artistic Renaissance is in part the story of the process by which artists gradually realized that Classicism represented another canon of taste and treated it accordingly.

But it is possible to suggest a more profound character to the change. Late Gothic has a peculiar aura of finality about it. From about 1470 to 1520, one gets the impression that the combination of decorative richness and realistic detail was being worked virtually to death. Classical antiquity at least provided an alternative form of art. It is arguable that change would have come in the north anyway and that adoption of Renaissance forms was a matter of coincidence and convenience. They were there at hand, for experiment.

The use of Renaissance forms was certainly encouraged, however, by the general admiration for Classical antiquity. They had a claim to "rightness" that led ultimately to the abandonment of all Gothic forms as being barbarous. This development belongs to the history of the Italian Renaissance, but the phenomenon emphasizes one aspect of medieval art. Through all the changes of Romanesque and Gothic, no body of critical literature appeared in which people tried to evaluate the art and distinguish old from new, good from bad. The development of such a literature was part of the Renaissance and, as such, was intimately related to the defense of Classical art. This meant that Gothic art was left in an intellectually defenseless state. All the praise went to ancient art, most of the blame to the art of the more recent past. Insofar as Gothic art had no critical literature by which a part of it, at least, could be justified, it was, to that extent, inarticulate.

CHAPTER FOUR

RENAISSANCE ARCHITECTURE

About 1400 a great change took place in society and culture in Italy. As it evolved it came to be called the Renaissance, or "rebirth," because of the rediscovery of ancient Roman literature and art in the period. This was, however, only one of its aspects, and many would say only a minor one. First of all, it was the moment of the discovery of individuality, of people able to think and act for themselves. The medieval worker had been an anonymous toiler for the glory of God. On the medieval facade of the church of St. Hubert in Troyes, one reads *non nobis, Domine, non nobis, sed nomini tuo da gloriam*—"Not to us, O Lord, not to us, but to your name be glory." But one reads across the front of the Renaissance church of San Francesco in Rimini simply the name of the ruler who built it, Sigismondo Malatesta, and the

The Tempio Malatestiano in Rimini, Italy, was converted, beginning in 1446, from the Gothic-style Church of San Francesco according to the plans of the early Renaissance Florentine architect Leon Battista Alberti.

date. The building came to be called Tempio Malatestiano, the Temple of Malatesta.

The Renaissance individual, freed from medieval superstition, cynically experimented in politics (as can be seen in Niccolò Machiavelli's book *Il Principe* [*The Prince*] of 1513), explored new areas of science and nature (as did Galileo), conceived a new philosophy—Neoplatonism—that combined Christian and ancient thought, reintroduced realism into painting and sculpture, and created a new style in architecture. The Renaissance architect was a new and different sort. In place of the medieval craftsman-architect, there were now men skilled in all artistic media, men who understood theory as well as practice and who pretended to personal worth and even genius. Among the leading architects of the period were two sculptors—Filippo Brunelleschi and Michelangelo. Leon Battista Alberti and Andrea Palladio wrote treatises on architecture. To these men architecture was not a mechanical art pursued by traditional craft rules but a liberal art controlled by abstract intellectual speculation.

PROPORTION AND BEAUTY

The concept of the Renaissance, which aimed to achieve the rebirth or re-creation of ancient Classical culture, originated in Florence in the early 15th century and then spread throughout most of the Italian peninsula; by the end of the 16th century, the new style pervaded almost all of Europe, gradually replacing the Gothic style of the late Middle Ages. It encouraged a revival of naturalism, seen in Italian 15th-century painting and sculpture, and of Classical forms and ornament in architecture, such as the column and round arch, the tunnel vault, and the dome.

Knowledge of the Classical style in architecture was derived during the Renaissance from two sources: the ruins of ancient Classical buildings, particularly in Italy but also in France and Spain, and the treatise *De architectura* (c. 27 BCE; "On Architecture") by Roman architect Vitruvius. For Classical antiquity and, therefore, for the Renaissance, the basic element of architectural design was the order, a system of traditional architectural units. During the Renaissance five orders were used—Tuscan, Doric, Ionic, Corinthian, and Composite—with various ones prevalent in different periods. For example, the ornate, decorative quality of the Corinthian order was embraced during the early Renaissance, while the masculine simplicity and strength of the Doric was preferred during the Italian High Renaissance. Following ancient Roman practice (e.g., the Colosseum or the Theatre of Marcellus), Renaissance architects often superimposed the order—that is, used a different order for each of the several stories of a building—commencing with the heavier, stronger Tuscan or Doric order below and then rising through the lighter, more decorative Ionic, Corinthian, and Composite.

Proportion during the Renaissance was the most important predetermining factor of beauty. On the authority of Vitruvius, the Renaissance architects found a harmony between the proportions of the human body and those of their architecture. There was even a relationship between architectural proportions and the Renaissance pictorial device of perspective. The concern of these architects for proportion led to the clear, measured expression and definition of architectural space and mass that differentiates the Renaissance style from the Gothic and encourages in the spectator an immediate and full comprehension of the building.

EARLY RENAISSANCE (1401-95)

The new state of architecture can be seen most clearly in Leon Battista Alberti. Medieval architects had risen from the anonymity of stonemasons, but Alberti was a gentleman and sportsman who practiced painting and music and who applied his general theorizing to architecture. In 1452 he wrote *De re aedificatoria* (*Ten Books on Architecture*), which was the first theoretical essay on building. Here he sought to rewrite Vitruvius "treatise on ancient Roman architecture to clarify and Christianize it as his philosopher friends in Florence were then rewriting and Christianizing the philosophy of Plato. Alberti conceived of architecture in terms of simple geometric volumes and numerical proportions, combining Plato's belief that beauty lies in numbers and Vitruvius" assertions that the orders were fixed in proportion. Alberti described an ideal city with all its streets laid out geometrically, centring on a cylindrical domed church set on a high base, with its windows placed far up the walls so that only the sky could be seen from inside. The church's decoration was to be very simple and its ornament to be faithfully copied from ancient Roman buildings.

Alberti's vision was a startlingly new one and a difficult one to realize. Alberti's young friend Filippo Brunelleschi had made the first attempt in his design for the church of San Lorenzo in Florence, begun in 1421. The plan is not centralized, but the dark stained glass and tall proportions of the Gothic style have been replaced by light, open regular spaces in the proportion of one to two. Greek columns and entablatures in dark gray stone define the spaces and measure the white stucco walls. Alberti had not yet written *De re aedificatoria* in 1421, but he was working on a treatise on perspective in painting, which was dedicated to Brunelleschi, and San Lorenzo seems to reflect Alberti's interest in the precise definition of space.

Alberti himself, beginning about the time of Brunelleschi's death in 1446, designed a number of buildings. Some were only exteriors added to existing structures, like the Tempio Malatestiano or the Rucellai Palace in Florence. He made the church facade in the form of a three-part Roman triumphal arch, intending that the tombs of Sigismondo Malatesta and his wife should be set on each side of the entrance opening. Alberti decorated the palace facade with a grid of Roman pilasters, setting up a proportional system followed also in the windows and doors. Two churches he later built in their entirety—San Andrea and San Sebastiano—were given pediments and pilasters surmounting broad flights of stairs like ancient Roman temples.

From Florence the early Renaissance style spread gradually over Italy, becoming prevalent in the second half of the 15th century. In the architecture of northern Italy there was a greater interest in pattern and colour. Colour was emphasized by the use of variegated marble inlays, as in the facade of the church of the Certosa di Pavia (begun 1491) or in most Venetian architecture. The favourite building material of northern Italy was brick with terra-cotta trim and decoration, a combination that created a pattern of light and dark over the entire building.

The emphasis on colour in northern Italian Renaissance architecture is exemplified by the marble inlays on the facade of the church of the Certosa di Pavia, a monastery in Ticinum.

On occasions when stone was used, as at the Palazzo Bevilacqua in Bologna (c. 1479–84), the blocks were cut with facets forming a diamond pattern on the facade. This decorative treatment, called rustication, affected the Classical orders. Classical pilasters often had panels of candelabra and arabesque decoration in delicate relief on the surfaces of their shafts; the lower third of a column was frequently carved with relief sculpture.

In Rome in the second half of the 15th century, there were several notable Renaissance palaces, principally derived from the style of Alberti, who spent extensive periods in Rome as a member of the papal court. The Palazzo Venezia (1455–1503) has a rather medieval exterior, but set within the palace is a characteristically Renaissance court (1468–71), of which only two sides forming an angle were completed. It has been suggested without definite proof that Alberti may have furnished the design for this court; it at least reveals his influence in its full understanding of the Classical style.

These examples of the early Renaissance in Rome were rapidly approaching the simplicity, monumentality, and massiveness of the High Renaissance of the early 16th century. Donato Bramante, who was to create this new style, was active in Lombardy in northern Italy, but his work in Milan, as at Santa Maria presso San Satiro (about 1480–86), was still in the Lombard early Renaissance manner. He was in contact at this time, however, with the great Florentine Leonardo da Vinci, who was active at the Milanese court. Leonardo was then considering the concept of the central-plan church and filling his notebooks with sketches of such plans, which Bramante must have studied. When Bramante moved to Rome at the very end of the 15th century, his study of ancient ruins—combined with the ideas of Leonardo and the growing classicism of Roman early Renaissance architecture—resulted in the flourishing of the High Renaissance.

HIGH RENAISSANCE (1495–1520)

Alberti moved from Florence to Rome about 1450. The power and the wealth of the pope at Rome were increasing, and about this time the centre of the Renaissance moved there. The years from 1503 to 1513 marked the glorious papacy of Julius II. He brought Michelangelo and Raphael to work for him in Rome, and in 1506 he commenced the huge project of rebuilding St. Peter's. The man he employed to replace the venerable but dilapidated basilica (built by the emperor Constantine) was

DONATO BRAMANTE

Donato Bramante (b. c. 1444, probably at Monte Asdrualdo, Duchy of Urbino [Italy]–d. April 11, 1514, Rome) began to paint early in life. "Besides reading and writing, he practiced much at the abacus," wrote an early biographer. In 1477 Bramante was working in Bergamo, painting architectural murals. Becoming known as a poet and an amateur musician, Bramante was also beginning to win acclaim as an architect and painter with a deep knowledge of perspective.

About 1477 Bramante left Bergamo and settled in the northern Italian province of Lombardy. He worked in various cities, finally moving to Milan. The first architectural design that can definitely be attributed to him dates to this period: a design representing a ruined temple with human figures. About the same time Bramante was working on the church of Santa Maria presso San Satiro in Milan, the first structure attributed to him. The crypt and lower portion of the cathedral of Pavia were probably done under his direction in 1488. Bramante worked with his close friend Leonardo da Vinci on stylistic and structural problems of the tiburio, or crossing tower, of the cathedral of Milan in about 1490.

Bramante's activities during the middle and late 1490s have not been well documented. He concentrated increasingly on designs for churches and abbeys. It is known, however, that in 1497 and 1498, he worked on the Cistercian monastery under construction in Milan. In this period he may have also studied the work of the architect Filippo Brunelleschi in Florence. Bramante moved to Rome in 1499 where he rose rapidly to prominence. Oliviero Carafa, the cardinal of Naples, commissioned the first work in Rome known to be Bramante's: the monastery and cloister of Santa Maria della Pace (finished in 1504). One of his finest works is the Tempietto di San Pietro in Montorio, intended to be the centre of a complex to mark the site where St. Peter was said to have been crucified.

Beginning in 1505, Bramante developed the plans for St. Peter's Basilica. The basilica ranks as his greatest work and was at that time one of the most ambitious building projects ever undertaken. Because he cleared the basilica site so thoroughly, Bramante became known as Maestro Ruinante (Master Wrecker). Named general superintendent of all papal construction

(continued on the next page)

(continued from the previous page)

under Pope Julius II, Bramante worked on the designs for the Belvedere at the Vatican and an enlargement of the church of Santa Maria del Popolo (both in Rome), as well as on various military fortifications.

Pope Julius wanted to re-create Rome as the artistic home of the ancient emperors. In Bramante's role as architect and town planner, he designed a huge new Palace of the Tribunes for the Via Giulia. His designs for the Palazzo Caprini—The House of Raphael—became the model for many 16th-century palaces.

Donato Bramante. Bramante was about 60 when he went to Rome from Milan, and he is supposed to have been trained as a painter by Piero della Francesca and Andrea Mantegna. While working as an architect in Milan, he would have known Leonardo, who was there at the time working out a series of geometric solutions for an ideal centralized church on Alberti's lines.

The Tempietto (1502), or small chapel, next to San Pietro in Montorio, typifies the new Renaissance style. Erected on the supposed site of the martyrdom of St. Peter, the Tempietto is circular in plan, with a colonnade of 16 columns surrounding a small cella, or enclosed interior sanctuary. The chapel was meant to stand in the centre of a circular court, which

The Tempietto, next to San Pietro in Montorio, Rome, designed by Donato Bramante, in 1502, which is remarkable for its elegantly simple reinterpretation of Classical forms.

brought to the Pope's mind the idea of rebuilding St. Peter's, which was in very poor condition. Bramante, therefore, prepared plans for a monumental church late in 1505, and in April 1506 the foundation stone was laid. Bramante's first design was a Greek cross in plan, with towers at the four corners and a tremendous dome over the crossing, inspired by that of the ancient Roman Pantheon but in this case raised on a drum. The Greek cross plan being unacceptable, Bramante finally planned to lengthen one arm to form a nave with a centralized crossing. At his death in 1514 Bramante had completed only the four main piers that were to support the dome, but these piers determined the manner in which later architects attempted the completion of the church.

Delay and confusion followed Julius's and Bramante's deaths within a year of each other, but in 1546 work was recommenced by Michelangelo, a worthy successor. He was 70 but had been executing architectural projects in Florence since the 1520s. His Medici Chapel in the church of San Lorenzo of 1520–34 and his Laurentian Library of 1523–59 were extraordinary for the expressive distortions of their details. Michelangelo extended these to his new design for St. Peter's. He simplified Bramante's composition, strengthened the proportions, and designed details as huge and powerful as the construction itself. He made the exterior wall to ripple in response to the intricate interior spaces as though they were pushing against an elastic membrane. He made its thickness palpable with deeply cut windows and niches and then held it together with a row of massive pilasters.

Several notable secular buildings were as important as the central-plan churches of this period. The largest palace of the High Renaissance is the Palazzo Farnese (1517–89) at Rome, designed and commenced by a follower of Bramante, Antonio da Sangallo the Younger, nephew of the older Sangallo. At Sangallo's death, in 1546, Michelangelo carried the palace toward completion, making important changes in the third story.

LATE RENAISSANCE AND ITALIAN MANNERISM (1520–1600)

"Mannerism" is the term applied to certain aspects of artistic style, mainly Italian, in the period between the High Renaissance of the early 16th century and the beginnings of Baroque art in the early 17th. Michelangelo's architecture shows an elaboration and expressiveness that might seem excessive and that has been called Mannerist. The painter Raphael lived to 1520, and, in his last works as well as in architectural designs done at the end of his life, he displayed architecture shows a greater emphasis on decorative qualities than on the expression of structural relationships.

After the resolved Classical order and measured harmony of Bramante's High Renaissance buildings, two main, though interwoven, directions of Mannerist development become apparent. One of these, emanating largely from Peruzzi, relied upon a detailed study of antique decorative motifs—grotesques, Classical gems, coins, and the like—which were used in a pictorial fashion to decorate the plane of the facade. This tendency was crystallized in Raphael's Palazzo Branconio dell'Aquila (destroyed) at Rome, where the regular logic of a Bramante facade was abandoned in favour of complex, out-of-step rhythms and encrusted surface decorations of medallions and swags. The detailed archaizing elements of this manner were taken up later by Pirro Ligorio, by the architects of the Palazzo Spada in Rome, and by Giovanni Antonio Dosio.

The second trend exploited the calculated breaking of rules, the taking of sophisticated liberties with Classical architectural vocabulary. Two very different buildings of the 1520s were responsible for initiating this taste, Michelangelo's Laurentian Library in Florence and the Palazzo del Te by Giulio Romano in Mantua. Michelangelo's composition relies upon a novel reassembly of Classical motifs for plastically expressive purposes, while Giulio's weird distortion of Classical forms is of a more consciously bizarre and entertaining kind. The various exterior aspects of the Palazzo del Te provide a succession of changing moods, which are contrived so as to retain the surprised attention of the spectator rather than to present him with a building that can be comprehended at a glance. In the courtyard the oddly fractured cornice sections create an air of ponderous tension, whereas the loggia is lightly elegant. Similarly, the illusionistic decoration of the interior runs the full gamut from heavy (if self-parodying) tragedy to pretty delicacy. Giulio also created a series of contrived vistas, through arches and doors, much like that later projected by Michelangelo for the Palazzo Farnese in Rome. Such management of scenic effects became one of the hallmarks of later Mannerist architecture.

With the works of northern Italian architects Galeazzo Alessi of Genoa, Leone Leoni of Milan, and Sebastiano Serlio of Bologna, Mannerist architecture gained a firm hold. In 1537 Serlio began to publish his series of books on architecture, in which he examined antiquity through Mannerist eyes and provided a series of pattern-book Mannerist designs. Three years later, Serlio joined the Italian Mannerist painter Francesco Primaticcio at Fontainebleau, where he helped to consolidate the early acceptance of Mannerist ideals in France. In the work

PALAZZO DEL TE

The Palazzo del Te, a palace now open to the public, located near Mantua, Italy, was constructed as the summer palace and horse farm of Duke Federico Gonzaga II. It was designed and built (*c.* 1525–35) by Giulio Romano, who also executed several of the fresco murals decorating the interior. The palace and its wall paintings are

This fresco can be seen on the east wall of the Sala di Psiche in the Palazzo del Te.

traditionally considered among the most important architectural expressions of Mannerism—especially in juxtaposed and displaced elements that create an effect of whimsy and motion. The building consists of a square block around a central court, with a splendid garden opening off at right angles to the main axis. The principal rooms are the Sala di Psiche, with erotic frescoes of the loves of the gods; the Sala dei Cavalli, with life-size portraits of some of the Gonzaga horses; and the fantastic Sala dei Giganti, a continuous scene, painted from floor to ceiling, of the giants attempting to storm Olympus and being repulsed by the gods.

of Alessandro Vittoria, the influence of central Italy was pronounced. His heavy ceiling moldings are composed of Classical motifs and bold strapwork. The north's taste for bizarre fancies—such as Vittoria's fireplace for the Palazzo Thiene—was often in advance of that in Rome and Florence.

Increasingly, architecture, sculpture, and walled gardens came to be regarded as part of a complex (but not unified) whole. In the Villa Giulia (c. 1550–55), the most significant secular project of its time, Vasari appears to have been in charge of the scenic integration of the various elements; Giacomo da Vignola designed part of the actual building, while the Mannerist sculptor Bartolommeo Ammanati was largely responsible for the sculptural decoration. In spite of the continuous stepped vista, the building makes its impact through a succession of diverse effects rather than by mounting up to a unified climax. There, and in Vasari's design for the Uffizi Palace (1560), the vista seems to have been based upon the supposed style of antique stage sets, as interpreted by Peruzzi. It is not surprising that the Venetian architect Andrea Palladio came closest to achieving a fully Mannerist style in his Teatro Olimpico at Vicenza, where the receding vistas and rich sculptural details create an effect of extraordinary complexity. Similarly, it is not surprising that the greatest of the later Mannerist architects in Florence, Bernardo Buontalenti, should have been an acknowledged master of stage design. He was employed at the Medici court as a designer of grandly fantastic ephemera—mock river battles and stage intermezzi (interval entertainments) in which elaborate stage machinery effected miraculous transformations, figures descending from the clouds to slay dragons that spouted realistic blood, followed by music and dance *all'antica*. As a garden designer, Buontalenti enriched the traditional formal schemes with entertaining diversions, in which water often played a prominent role—either in fountains or in wetting booby traps for the strolling visitor. Buontalenti's buildings possess much of this capricious spirit in addition to his brilliantly inventive command of fluently plastic detailing.

In their treatment of detail, 16th-century Florentine architects inevitably looked toward Michelangelo as their example of innovative genius. Michelangelo's Medici Chapel in San Lorenzo was executed, in Vasari's opinion, "in a style more varied and novel than that of any other master," and "thus all artists are under a great and eternal obligation to Michelangelo, seeing that he broke the fetters and chains that had earlier confined them to the creation of traditional forms." By Vasari's time the Mannerist quest for novelty had reached a thoroughly self-conscious level.

Michelangelo's later architecture in Rome was more restrained than his Florentine works. In 1546 he was commissioned to complete St. Peter's Basilica in Rome, succeeding Antonio da Sangallo the Younger. During the next 18 years he was able to complete most of his design for the church, except the facade and great dome above. He returned to a central-plan church reminiscent of Bramante's first project but with fewer parts. Michelangelo's elevation, still visible at the rear or sides of the church, is composed of gigantic pilasters and a rather high attic story. Between the pilasters are several stories of windows or niches. Unlike the harmonious orders and openings of the High Renaissance, these are constricted by the pilasters so that a tension is created in the wall surface. Michelangelo planned a tremendous semicircular dome on a drum as the climax of the composition. Engravings of his original project suggest that this dome would have been overwhelming in relation to the rest of the design. The great central dome was executed toward the end of the 16th century by Michelangelo's follower, Giacomo della Porta, who gave a more vertical expression to the dome by raising it about 25 feet (8 metres) higher than a semicircle. In the early 17th century, the Baroque architect Carlo Maderno added a large nave and facade to the front of the church, converting it into a Latin cross plan and destroying the dominating quality of the dome, at least from the exterior front.

This period of free and decorative Mannerism was followed by a more restrained Classical architecture seen to perfection in the work of one of the greatest architects of the Renaissance, Andrea Palladio. While Mannerism dominated Rome and central Italy, the rich island city of Venice and its region experienced in the work of Palladio the extension and final perfection of the balanced Neoplatonic architecture of Alberti and Bramante. Palladio had begun as a stonemason, but beginning about 1535 he was educated as a scholar by the literary reformer Giangiorgio Trissino. He later became a close friend of other scholars, most particularly the editor of Vitruvius,

The Villa Rotonda near Vicenza, Italy, was designed by Andrea Palladio in 1566–1571. It has Classical porticoes on each of its four sides.

Daniele Barbaro, and in 1555 Palladio became a founding member of the Accademia Olympica in Vicenza. In 1570 Palladio published his highly respected treatise, *I quattro libri dell'architettura* (*The Four Books of Architecture*). His work is remarkable for applying geometry and proportion as well as simplicity and correctness of precedent to all genres of architecture. He coordinated the proportions of every room in designs such as that for the Villa Rotonda near Vicenza of 1566–71. He also tried to apply the simple forms of the Roman temple—the evenly spaced rows of columns and the pediment—to both villas and churches, developing a uniquely satisfying type of church facade in San Giorgio Magno and Il Redentore in Venice. His buildings, especially as illustrated and described in his book, were to become the principal models of imitation as the Renaissance spread outward from Italy around 1600.

The most important architect of this period in Rome was Giacomo da Vignola, who wrote *Regola delli cinque ordini d'architettura* (1562; "Rule of the Five Orders of Architecture"), a treatise devoted solely to a consideration of the architectural orders and their proportions. Like Palladio's book, Vignola's *Regola* became a textbook for later Classical architecture. Of his many buildings, the project for the church of Il Gesù (1568) at Rome, the central church of the Jesuit order, was very influential on the later history of architecture. The plan is a Latin cross with side chapels flanking the nave, but the eastern end is a central plan, capped by a dome. Il Gesù's plan was imitated throughout Europe, but especially in Italy, during the early Baroque period of the 17th century. Vignola built the church except for its facade, which was executed by Giacomo della Porta. Della Porta, inspired by Vignola's original design, created a facade concentrated toward its centre, which, like the plan, was the prototype for most early Baroque facades of the late 16th and 17th centuries.

CHAPTER FIVE

BAROQUE AND ROCOCO

About 1600, European culture was again revolutionized. In northern Europe the Renaissance gave way to the Protestant Reformation. In Italy, beginning with the foundation of the Jesuit Order in 1539 and the Council of Trent of 1545–63, the Roman Catholic church began the Counter-Reformation, a campaign to strengthen itself in reaction. There resulted a more purely Catholic and emotional style, the Baroque.

Italy, however, was becoming less and less the centre of European civilization. The discovery of America brought great wealth to Spain in the 16th century; the expansion of trade made Holland and Britain major powers in the centuries following; and political centralization made France under Louis XIV the most influential state on the Continent. In these northern states religious architecture was overshadowed by political building—

palaces and government institutions. The profession of architecture evolved in response. The architect had become a gentleman during the Renaissance. Now he became a government official, a bureaucrat, a part of the centralized administration of building. The greatest architects of the age—Jules Hardouin-Mansart, Sir Christopher Wren, Jacques-Germain Soufflot, Balthasar Neumann—were heads of corps of designers and builders who were assembled to carry out national construction projects of all sorts. These were educated men, but they were not (with the exception of Wren) philosophers or (with the exception of Bernini) practitioners of many arts.

HISTORICAL CONTEXT

During the Baroque period (*c.* 1600–1750), architecture, painting, and sculpture were integrated into decorative ensembles. Architecture and sculpture became pictorial, and painting became illusionistic. Baroque art was essentially concerned with the dramatic and the illusory, with vivid colours, hidden light sources, luxurious materials, and elaborate, contrasting surface textures used to heighten immediacy and sensual delight. Ceilings

This interior view of the church of San Lorenzo (1666–79) in Turin, Italy, shows painted scenes typical of Baroque churches, which were designed to direct the attention of the worshippers upward toward heaven.

of Baroque churches, dissolved in painted scenes, presented vivid views of the infinite to the worshiper and directed him through his senses toward heavenly concerns. Seventeenth-century Baroque architects made architecture a means of propagating faith in the church and in the state. Baroque palaces expanded to command the infinite and to display the power and order of the state. Baroque space, with directionality, movement, and positive molding, contrasted markedly with the static, stable, and defined space of the High Renaissance and with the frustrating conflict of unbalanced spaces of the preceding Mannerist period. Baroque space invited participation and provided multiple changing views. Renaissance space was passive and invited contemplation of its precise symmetry. While a Renaissance statue was meant to be seen in the round, a Baroque statue either had a principal view with a preferred angle or was enclosed by a niche or frame. A Renaissance building was to be seen equally from all sides, while a Baroque building had a main axis or viewpoint as well as subsidiary viewpoints. Attention was focused on the entrance axis or on the central pavilion, and its symmetry was emphasized by the central culmination. A Baroque building expanded in its effect to include the square facing it, and often the ensemble included all the buildings on the square as well as the approaching streets and the surrounding landscape. Baroque buildings dominated their environment; Renaissance buildings separated themselves from it.

The Baroque rapidly developed into two separate forms: the strongly Roman Catholic countries (Italy, Spain, Portugal, Flanders, Bohemia, southern Germany, Austria, and Poland) tended toward freer and more active architectural forms and surfaces; in Protestant regions (England, the Netherlands, and the remainder of northern Europe) architecture was more

ITALY

The first great Baroque architect was the Italian Gian Lorenzo Bernini. He was the last Renaissance architect in the sense that he was equally able in sculpture, painting, and building. But already there was a difference; instead of being a free-thinking Humanist like Alberti or Leonardo, Bernini was a faithful Catholic and a lay member of the Jesuit Order. This was reflected in his works, which were stage sets for the dramatization of Catholic ritual.

His first architectural work was the remodeled Church of Santa Bibiana in Rome. At the same time, Bernini was commissioned to build a symbolic structure over the tomb of St. Peter in St. Peter's Basilica in Rome. The result is the famous immense gilt-bronze baldachin executed between 1624 and 1633. Its twisted columns derive from the early Christian columns that had been used in the altar screen of Old St. Peter's. Bernini's most original contribution to the final work is the upper framework of crowning volutes flanked by four angels that supports the orb and cross. The baldachin is perfectly proportioned to its setting, and one hardly realizes that it is as tall as a four-story building. Its lively outline moving upward to the triumphant crown, its dark colour heightened with burning gold, give it the character of a living organism. An unprecedented fusion of sculpture and architecture, the baldachin is the first truly Baroque monument. It ultimately formed the centre of a programmatic decoration designed by Bernini for the interior of St. Peter's.

In his later years, the growing desire to control the environments of his statuary led Bernini to concentrate more and more on architecture. Of the churches he designed after completing the Cornaro Chapel, the most impressive is that of Sant'Andrea al Quirinale (1658–70) in Rome, with its dramatic high altar, soaring dome, and unconventionally sited oval plan. But Bernini's greatest architectural achievement is the colonnade enclosing the piazza before St. Peter's Basilica. The chief function of the large space was to hold the crowd that gathered for the papal benediction on Easter and other special occasions.

Bernini had a brilliant assistant, Francesco Borromini, who in the 1630s emerged as his competitor in architecture. If Bernini's designs appear dramatic, Borromini's seem bizarre. His largest work, the chapel of San Ivo della Sapienza in the Collegio Romano of 1642–60 displays a distorted triangular space internally and a stepped dome that culminates in a spiral on the exterior. His intentions were evidently symbolic. The plan shows the triangular emblem of divine wisdom, and the spiral evokes the pillar of truth. The whole building has thus been made to become the Domus Sapientiae, the "House of Wisdom," expressive of its location in a college and its dedication to a saint of learning.

At the end of the 17th century, Bernini's use of dramatic lighting and Borromini's free spatial geometry were combined by Guarino Guarini in a series of churches in Turin. Here space opens mysteriously behind space, and webs of dome ribs seem to float in front of bursts of divine light, producing the highest expression of the Italian baroque.

Filippo Juvarra's Palazzo Madama, Turin (1718–21), has one of the most spectacular of all Baroque staircases, but the true heir to Guarini was Bernardo Vittone. To increase the vertical effect and the unification of space in churches such as Santa Chiara, Brà (1742), Vittone raised the main arches, eliminated the drum, and designed a double dome in which one could look through spherical openings puncturing the inner dome and see the outer shell painted with images of saints and angels: a glimpse of heaven.

The staircase of the Palazzo Madama in Turin, Italy, now the home of the Museum of Ancient Arts, is a fine example of Baroque architecture.

SPAIN

The Spanish Empire in the 16th and 17th centuries enjoyed great prosperity as well as close proximity and political interrelationship with Italy. In 1563–84 there arose the first great non-Italian work of the High Renaissance, Philip II's Escorial. It was simultaneously a monastery, mausoleum, fortress, and palace—a symbol of royal piety and power that became characteristic of the age. The principal architect, Juan de Herrera, worked closely with the king. The result, built in black granite, has the clarity of Bramante and the massiveness of Michelangelo and achieves the king's desire that it have "simplicity of form, severity in the whole, nobility without arrogance, majesty without ostentation."

Spanish Baroque was similar to Italian Baroque but with a greater emphasis on surface decorations. Alonso Cano, in his facade of the Granada Cathedral (1667), and Eufrasio López de Rojas, with the facade of the cathedral of Jaén (1667), show Spain's absorption of the concepts of the Baroque at the same time that it maintained a local tradition. The greatest of the Spanish masters was José Benito Churriguera, whose work shows most fully the Spanish Baroque interest in surface texture and decorative detail. His lush ornamentation attracted many followers, and Spanish architecture of the late 17th century and early 18th century has been labeled "Churrigueresque." Narciso and Diego Tomé, in the University of Valladolid (1715), and Pedro de Ribera, in the facade of the San Fernando Hospital (now the Municipal Museum) in Madrid (1722), proved themselves to be the chief inheritors of Churriguera.

Another outstanding figure of 18th-century Spanish architecture was Ventura Rodríguez, who, in his designs for the Chapel of Our Lady of Pilar in the cathedral of Saragossa (1750), showed himself to be a master of the developed Rococo in its altered Spanish form; but it was a Fleming, Jaime Borty Miliá, who brought Rococo to Spain when he built the west front of the cathedral of Murcia in 1733.

FRANCE

France equaled Spain in power and finally, during the reign of Louis XIV (1643–1715), outshone its rival. The Renaissance had arrived early there also, during the reign of Francis I (1494–1547) in his palace at Fontainebleau. He had imported Italian artists, including Leonardo (who died at Amboise in 1519), but the architectural results during the 16th century were largely decorative and fantastic. In 1615, however, an equivalent to the Escorial began to rise in Paris in the Luxembourg Palace designed by Solomon de Brosse for the regent

Marie de Médicis. This was followed by the châteaux and churches of François Mansart, especially his Val de Grace of 1645–67, and by the whole town and château of the Cardinal Richelieu commenced to a single design by Jacques Lemercier in 1631.

It was Louis XIV, upon his accession to power in 1661, who carried the combined expression of central power and state church to a new plane. He started by projecting the completion of his city palace, the Louvre, and in 1664 invited Bernini to Paris to execute it. But what had started as an admission of Italian supremacy ended as an assertion of French independence when Bernini returned to Rome after a few months' stay, and his baroque project was superseded by a simpler, more correct one by Claude Perrault, executed from 1667 to 1670.

Paris, however, was becoming too small a canvas for Louis XIV's architectural display of royal authority. His superintendent of finances, Nicolas Fouquet, had employed in 1657–61 the architect Louis Le Vau, the painter Charles Le Brun, and the landscape gardener André Le Nôtre to coordinate their three arts to produce his château at Vaux-le-Vicomte. Louis was deeply impressed. He had Fouquet's finances investigated, took over his team of artists, and in 1668 set them to work producing an even grander ensemble for him at Versailles. Here huge expanses of formal gardens on one side and three monumental avenues on the other culminate in a vast palace designed in the severe style of the Louvre and the Escorial. By serving as a model for Louis XIV's Palace of Versailles, the complex at Vaux was perhaps the most important mid-century European palace.

Versailles was built slowly in parts. Le Vau, Le Nôtre, and Le Brun began working at Versailles within a few years of their success at Vaux, but the major expansion of the palace did not occur until after the end of the Queen's War (1668). At Versailles, Le Vau showed his ability to deal with a building of imposing size. The simplicity of his forms and the rich, yet restrained, articulation of the garden facade mark Versailles as his most accomplished building. Le Nôtre's inventive disposition of ground, plant, and water forms created a wide range of vistas, terraces, gardens, and wooded areas that integrated palace and landscape into an environment emphasizing

The extensive gardens at the Palace of Versailles, France, designed by André Le Nôtre, are as remarkable as the grand buildings.

the delights of continuity and separation, of the infinite and the intimate. Upon Le Vau's death in 1670, Jules Hardouin-Mansart took over, designing the famous Galérie des Glaces (begun 1678). He proved himself equal to Louis XIV's desires by more than trebling the size of the palace (1678–1708). Versailles became the palatial ideal and model throughout Europe and the Americas until the end of the 18th century. A succession of grand palaces was built, including Castle Howard and Blenheim Palace, in England (1699; 1705–25), by Sir John Vanbrugh; the Residenz of Würzburg, Germany (1719), by Neumann; the Zwinger in Dresden, Germany (1711), by Matthäus Daniel Pöppelmann; the Belvedere, Vienna (1714), by Johann Lukas von Hildebrandt; the Royal Palace, Caserta, Italy (1752), by Luigi Vanvitelli; and the Royal Palace (National Palace) at Madrid (1736), by Giovanni Battista Sacchetti.

Hardouin-Mansart rose to be first royal architect and then, in 1699, superintendent des bâtiments (superintendent of buildings). He designed Louis XIV's last and largest projects in a style that finally began to show baroque complexity and richness—the Château de Marly (begun 1679), the Dôme des Invalides (Paris, 1679–91, intended as Louis's mausoleum), and the Place Vendôme (Paris, begun 1698). His Dôme des Invalides

PALACE OF VERSAILLES

The Palace of Versailles, former French royal residence and centre of government, is now a national landmark. It is located in the city of Versailles, Yvelines *département*, Île-de-France *région*, northern France, 10 miles (16 km) west-southwest of Paris. As the centre of the French court, Versailles was one of the grandest theatres of European absolutism.

The original residence, built from 1631 to 1634, was primarily a hunting lodge and private retreat for Louis XIII (reigned 1610-43) and his family. Under the guidance of Louis XIV (1643-1715), it was transformed (1661-1710) into an immense and extravagant complex surrounded by stylized English and French gardens; every detail of its construction glorified the king. The additions were designed by such renowned architects as Jules Hardouin-Mansart, Robert de Cotte, and Louis Le Vau. Charles Le Brun oversaw the interior decoration. Landscape artist André Le Nôtre created symmetrical French gardens that included ornate fountains with "magically" still water, expressing the power of humanity—and, specifically, the king—over nature.

(continued on the next page)

(continued from the previous page)

Declared the official royal residence in 1682 and the official residence of the court of France on May 6, 1682, the Palace of Versailles was abandoned after the death of Louis XIV in 1715. In 1722, however, it was returned to its status as royal residence. Further additions were made during the reigns of Louis XV (1715–74) and Louis XVI (1774–92). Following the French Revolution of 1789, the complex was nearly destroyed; it was subsequently restored by Louis-Philippe (1830–48), but its utility gradually decreased. By the 20th century, though it was occasionally used for plenary congresses of the French parliament or as housing for visiting heads of state, the primary utility of the palace lay in tourism.

Among the most famous rooms in the palace are the Galerie des Glaces (Hall of Mirrors; 1678–89) and the other Grands Appartements (State Rooms). The former is characterized by 17 wide, arcaded mirrors opposite 17 windows; glass chandeliers hang from its arched, ornately painted ceiling, and gilded statues and reliefs border its walls. The hall is flanked on opposite ends by the equally striking Salon de la Paix (Salon of Peace) and

Salon de la Guerre (Salon of War). It was in the Galerie des Glaces that the Treaty of Versailles was signed by the Allies and Germany in 1919. Other important sites are the Grand Trianon (1678–88) and the late 18th-century Petit Trianon, which were built as private residences for the royal family and special guests. The Museum of French History, founded in 1837 during the period of restoration overseen by Louis-Philippe, was consecrated "to all the glories of France"; however, its 6,000 paintings and 2,000 sculptures are largely closed to the public.

UNESCO designated the palace and its gardens a World Heritage site in 1979. Following a devastating winter storm in 1989, which destroyed more than 1,000 trees on the palace grounds, the French government initiated a wide-ranging project of repair and renovation. A severe windstorm in 1999 caused the loss of some 10,000 trees, including several planted by Marie Antoinette and Napoleon Bonaparte. The chateau was also damaged. In the late 1990s some nine million people visited the palace annually.

is generally agreed to be the finest church of the last half of the 17th century in France. The correctness and precision of its form, the harmony and balance of its spaces, and the soaring vigour of its dome make it a landmark not only of the Paris skyline but also of European Baroque architecture. Significantly, Hardouin-Mansart was one of the first architects to be accused by his contemporaries of not producing his own designs but of using the talents of skillful assistants.

After interior designer Nicolas Pineau returned to France from Russia, he, with architects Gilles-Marie Oppenordt and Juste-Aurèle Meissonier, who were increasingly concerned with asymmetry, realized the full Rococo. Meissonier and Oppenordt should be noted too for their exquisite, imaginative architectural designs that were unfortunately never built (e.g., Meissonier's facade of Saint-Sulpice, Paris, 1726).

The early years of the 18th century saw the artistic centre of Europe shift from Rome to Paris. Pierre Lepautre, working under Hardouin-Mansart on the interiors of the Château de Marly, invented new decorative ideas that became the Rococo. Lepautre changed the typical late 17th-century flat arabesque, which filled a geometrically constructed panel, to a linear pattern in relief, which was enclosed by a frame that determined its own shape. White-and gold-painted 17th-century interiors (e.g., the central salon of the palace at Versailles) were replaced by varnished natural-wood surfaces (e.g., Château de Meudon, Cabinet à la Capucine) or by painted pale greens, blues, and creams (e.g., Cabinet Vert, Versailles, 1735). The resulting delicate asymmetry in relief and elegant freedom revolutionized interior decoration and within a generation exerted a profound effect on architecture. Architects rejected the massive heavy relief of the Baroque in favour of a light and delicate, but still active, surface. Strong, active, and robust interior spaces gave way to intricate, elegant but restrained spatial sequences.

HOLY ROMAN EMPIRE

To the east of France lay the Holy Roman Empire with its capital at Vienna. Beginning in 1690, Johann Bernhard Fischer von Erlach worked there, starting the baroque Karlskirche in 1716. The most extraordinary work in the German sphere was produced in the early 18th century in the bishopric of Würzburg, where Balthasar Neumann, trained locally as a military engineer, served as state architect. He designed the magnificent bishop's Residenz (palace), with ceiling frescoes by Giovanni Battista Tiepolo, as well as the pilgrimage church of Vierzehnheiligen (1741–71, near Lichtenfels in Bavaria). In the latter building the spatial geometry of Borromini is combined with a richness of decoration and an openness of structure that make the whole space a religious apparition.

ENGLAND

France's real competitor for domination of northern Europe, however, was the developing maritime nation of England. The Renaissance had arrived especially late there. After an almost abortive introduction of Palladianism by Inigo Jones in the early 17th century, the development was suspended until Sir Christopher Wren's appointment as surveyor of the king's works in 1669. He was the last scholar-architect, having pursued mathematics and astronomy before becoming involved in building. He became one of the most brilliant and prolific architect-bureaucrats of the age. Before his death in 1723 he had designed 52

London churches (after the 1666 fire), carried through the construction of St. Paul's Cathedral from foundation to cupola-top between 1673 and 1710, extended several palaces, and built two huge military hospitals at Chelsea and Greenwich.

The dome of St. Paul's Cathedral, one of the most notable features of the structure, still rises over the city of London, England.

ST. PAUL'S CATHEDRAL

St. Paul's Cathedral is located in central London on a site with a troubled past. A Roman temple to Diana may once have stood on the site, but the first Christian cathedral there was dedicated to St. Paul in 604, during the rule of King Aethelberht I. That cathedral burned, and its replacement (built 675–685) was destroyed by Viking raiders in 962. In 1087 a third cathedral erected on the site also burned.

The fourth cathedral, now known as Old St. Paul's, was constructed beginning in the late 11th century. After the edifice fell into disrepair in the late 16th century, major repairs were initiated in the 1630s by Inigo Jones. During the English Civil Wars (1642–51), however, the structure was severely damaged by Cromwellian cavalry troops who used it as a barracks. In the 1660s Christopher Wren was enlisted to survey and repair the cathedral, but it was destroyed in the Great Fire of London (1666) before work could begin. Wren subsequently designed and oversaw the construction of the present cathedral, which was built mainly of Portland stone. His plans were approved in 1675, and work was carried out until 1710.

Wren's design combined Neoclassical, Gothic, and Baroque elements in an attempt to symbolize the ideals of both the English Restoration and 17th-century scientific philosophy. His finished cathedral differed greatly from the plan approved in 1675, however. Wren apparently based many of his modifications on an earlier (1672–73), unapproved plan for St. Paul's, which was first given shape in his 20-foot-long "Great Model," now kept on display in the cathedral's trophy room.

St. Paul's famous dome, which has long dominated the London skyline, is composed of three shells: an outer dome, a concealed brick cone for structural support, and an inner dome. The cross atop its outer dome stands nearly 366 feet (112 metres) above ground level (some 356 feet [109 metres] above the main floor of the cathedral). Below the cross are an 850-ton lantern section and the outer, lead-encased dome, both of which are supported by the brick cone. At the base of the lantern (the apex of the outer dome) is the famous Golden Gallery, which offers panoramas of London some 530 steps (and some 280 feet [85 metres]) above ground. Farther down, at a point just below the brick cone, is the Stone Gallery, another popular viewing spot.

(continued on the next page)

(continued from the previous page)

The frescoes and grisaille of the inner dome are best admired from the Whispering Gallery (so called because a whisper from one side of the gallery can be heard from the other side), 99 feet (30 metres) above the cathedral floor. To the north and south of the dome section are wide transepts, each with semicircular porticoes; to the east lie the choir and the Jesus Chapel, while the nave and the "front" entrance are to the west.

There are some 300 monuments within the cathedral. Many notable soldiers, artists, and intellectuals have been buried in the crypt, including Lord Nelson, the duke of Wellington, and Wren himself, who was one of the first to be entombed there.

Wren is chiefly remembered for St. Paul's Cathedral. It is French in its severity but original in its Gothic plan (insisted upon by the cathedral chapter) and ingenious in its vaulting and dome. From Wren's office emerged Nicholas Hawksmoor who, together with the gentleman-architect Sir John Vanbrugh, erected a series of huge ducal palaces in the early 18th century, notably Blenheim Palace near Oxford (begun 1705).

France continued in the 18th century to be the centre of northern European culture and architecture, producing Ange-Jacques Gabriel's Place de la Concorde (begun 1757) and Jacques-Germain Soufflot's Panthéon (1755–92). The latter structure was built originally as the church of Ste-Geneviève, and all of its complication of colonnades, domes, and windows restates the original Renaissance theme of the centralized, vaulted space that is decorated with sober ancient Roman ornamentation.

NORTH AMERICA

The colonial architecture of the United States and Canada was as diverse as the peoples who settled there: English, Dutch, French, Swedish, Spanish, German, Scots-Irish. Each group carried with it the style and building customs of the mother country, adapting them as best it could to the materials and conditions of a new land. Thus, there were several colonial styles. The earliest buildings of all but the Spanish colonists were medieval in style: not the elaborate Gothic of the great European cathedrals and manor houses but the simple late Gothic of village houses and barns. These practical structures were well adapted to the pioneer conditions that prevailed in the colonies until about 1700, and few changes were needed to adapt them to the more severe climate. The styles were frank expressions of functional and structural requirements, with only an occasional bit of ornament. So far as is known, no single new structural technique or architectural form was invented in the North American colonies.

There were seven reasonably distinct regional colonial styles:

1. The New England colonial, visible in almost 100 surviving 17th-century houses, was predominantly of wood construction with hand-hewn oak frames and clapboard siding; its prototypes are to be found chiefly in the southeastern counties of England.
2. The Dutch colonial, centring in the Hudson River Valley, in western Long Island, and in northern New Jersey, made more use of stone and brick or a combination of these with wood; its prototypes were in Holland and Flanders. The style persisted in this region until after the American Revolution.
3. The Swedish colonial settlement, established in 1638 along the lower Delaware River, was of short duration but contributed the log cabin (in the sense of a structure with round logs, notched at

the corners and with protruding ends) to American architecture.

4. The Pennsylvania colonial style was late in origin (the colony was not founded until 1681) and rapidly developed into a sophisticated Georgian mode, based on English precedents. A local variant, often called Pennsylvania Dutch, evolved in the southeastern counties where Germans settled in large numbers after 1710.

5. The Southern colonial flourished in Maryland, Virginia, and the Carolinas. Story-and-a-half brick houses, sometimes with large projecting end chimneys and decorative brick masonry, prevailed.

6. The French colonial, stemming from medieval French sources, evolved in Canada in the Maritime Provinces and the St. Lawrence Valley. The earliest impressive structure was the habitation of the French explorer Samuel de Champlain, built at Port Royal, Nova Scotia, in 1604. Most of the surviving early houses of New France are to be found in the province of Quebec. The French settled the Great Lakes and Mississippi regions by the late 17th century and introduced the Quebec style. Far to the south, Louisiana was established

as a colony in 1699, and New Orleans became the capital in 1718. There grew up a distinctive regional style in the close-packed streets of the Vieux Carré of New Orleans and in the quiet plantations of the bayou country.

7. The Spanish colonial style in the United States extended geographically and chronologically from St. Augustine in 1565 to San Francisco in 1848. The five great mission fields were in Florida, New Mexico (from 1598), Texas, Arizona (both from 1690), and California (from 1769). Unlike other colonial styles, which were essentially medieval, the Spanish colonial followed the Renaissance and Baroque styles of Spain and Mexico.

The architectural style of the 18th century in England and in the English colonies in America was called Georgian. There are slight differences in usages of the term in the two countries. In England, Georgian refers to the mode in architecture and the allied arts of the reigns of George I, II, and III, extending from 1714 to 1820. In America, Georgian refers to the architectural style of the English colonies from about 1700 to the American Revolution in the late 1770s. Formal and aristocratic in spirit, it was at first based on the Baroque work of Sir Christopher Wren and his English followers; but after 1750 it became more severely Palladian. Typically, houses were of red brick with white-painted wood trim. Interiors had central halls, elaborately turned stair balustrades, paneled walls painted in warm colours and white plaster ceilings. All of these features were new to the colonies in 1700. Some of the earliest Georgian buildings were at Williamsburg, capital of Virginia from 1699 to 1780; other notable examples are Independence Hall, Philadelphia (1745), and King's Chapel, Boston (1750). The style was followed by the Federal style, 1780–1820.

CHAPTER SIX

TRENDS IN ARCHITECTURE FROM *c.* 1750 TO 1900

Jacques-Germain Soufflot's Panthéon was not only the culmination of the baroque tradition but also the first hint of the future course of architecture. It shows a growing awareness of the possibility of achieving pictorial effects. The building uses an ingenious hidden system of Gothic buttresses, which make possible the high windows that bring light streaming through the layers of columns and arches, which, in turn, support the roof vaults. The interior of the Panthéon is dramatized in much the same way as Soufflot's contemporary, the Italian engraver Giovanni Battista Piranesi, dramatized his views of ancient Roman monuments and buildings.

Piranesi's engravings influenced many architects in France and England and helped to begin a movement toward what has been called Romantic Classicism, or

Neoclassicism. Classical forms began to be put together for dramatic and expressive effect rather than purely to create orderly compositions. With the writings of the theorist Marc-Antoine Laugier in France, architecture began to be seen as originating in natural rather than human form, and architects began to try to recreate the effect of landscape in their works. This point of view paralleled the thinking of philosophers like Jean-Jacques Rousseau, who saw nature as the source of mankind's fundamental character. About the time of the French Revolution, the architect Étienne-Louis Boullée worked on projects for buildings that were intended to evoke natural phenomena such as the four seasons through their forms and character.

Many of Boullée's projects also reflected a popular philosophical concept, that of the sublime, which was put forward by the Englishman Edmund Burke in 1756 in his *Philosophical Inquiry into Our Ideas of the Sublime and Beautiful in Art.* Burke tried to categorize the natural effects that combined to make something sublime; that is, those that are impressive beyond the normal range of experience. An offshoot of his theory was the development of the concept of the picturesque, which was based on a painter's interpretation of nature. The picturesque caught the imagination of architects, particularly in England, where the ancient form of the Roman villa was now freely adapted to suburban and country houses with features such as asymmetrical towers. A system of purposely irregular landscaping, whose best known practitioner was Humphrey Repton, was developed to complement these houses.

NEOCLASSICISM

The classicism that flourished in the period 1750–1830 is often known as "Neoclassicism," in order to distinguish it, perhaps unnecessarily, from the Classical architecture of ancient Rome or of the Renaissance. The search for intellectual and architectural truth characterized the period. (In the 18th century, modern classicism was described as the "true style," the word "Neoclassical" being then unknown.) Stylistically this began with an onslaught against Baroque architecture, which—with its emphasis on illusion and applied ornament—was felt to be manifestly untruthful. Renaissance architecture was also questioned. As early as the 1680s the French architect Claude Perrault had undermined the Renaissance concept of the absolute right of the orders. According to Perrault, the proportions of the orders had no basis in absolute truth but were instead the result of fancy and association. The consequent attempt to discover a new basis for architectural reality took many forms, from archaeology to theory.

Essentially representing a new taste for Classical serenity and archaeologically correct forms, 18th-century classicism manifested itself in all the arts. It corresponded to a new attitude toward the past that began to be perceptible about 1750; it was at once a reaction against the last phase of the Baroque and symptomatic of a new philosophical outlook. As the Baroque was the style of absolutism, so Neoclassicism corresponded loosely with the Enlightenment and the Age of Reason. Coincidental with the rise of Neoclassicism and exerting a formative and profound influence on the movement at all stages was a new and more scientific interest in Classical antiquity. The discovery, exploration, and archaeological investigation of Classical sites in Italy, Greece, and Asia Minor were crucial to the emergence of Neoclassicism.

The emergence of the science of archaeology was indicative of a new attitude to the past in which separate and distinct chronological periods could be distinguished. This sense of a plurality of valid styles replaced the older conception of Classical Rome as the unique object of veneration. An important architectural corollary of this idea, which was to spring into prominence in the 19th century, was the notion of a modern style of building. Just as the past could now be interpreted and re-created by the study of a diverse range of monuments, each now seeming to be uniquely characteristic of its own particular moment in time, so it was thought possible that a mode of building reflecting the present, a mode recognizable by future archaeologists as uniquely representative of their own time, might be created.

Numerous events beginning in the second decade of the 18th century, when English tourists began to visit Italy to experience, explore, and collect fragments of its antique past, herald this new and increasing interest in archaeology. As early as 1719, Bernard de Montfaucon, a French antiquarian, began to publish his 10-volume *L'Antiquité expliquée et représentée en figures* (1719; *Antiquity Explained and Represented in Diagrams*, 1721–25). It was an immediate success. Excavations at the newly discovered ancient cities of Pompeii and Herculaneum (discovered in 1719) began in 1748 and 1738, respectively. The publication of the Comte de Caylus's *Recueil d'antiquités*, which began to appear in 1752, was another landmark. Influential plates of Roman antiquities drawn by Piranesi first appeared in 1743, when he published his book of etched plates entitled *Prima parte di architettura*. A steady stream of similar works followed from Piranesi's workshop. The first of a long and significant list of publications of measured drawings and picturesque views of Roman and Greek antiquities was Robert Wood's *Ruins of Palmyra* (1753), which was followed in 1757 by the same author's *Ruins of Balbec* and by the *Ruins of the Palace of the Emperor Diocletian at Spalatro in Dalmatia*, written in 1764 by the English Neoclassical architect and designer Robert Adam.

At the same time a significant interest in Greek antiquities was emerging along with a growing belief in the superiority of Greek over Roman architecture that was to result in a Greek Revival in architecture. At about this time the 6th-century Greek ruins at Paestum in southern Italy and in Sicily began to attract the attention of visitors. The Paestum sites were first described by the Italian artist Domenico Antonini in 1745. In 1750 French architect Soufflot visited Paestum. The following year Giuseppe Maria Pancraz's *Antichità siciliane* appeared, and in 1769 the architect Gabriel-Pierre-Martin Dumont's *Ruines de Paestum* was published. The picturesque qualities of these Greek temples, with their heavy baseless columns broken and overgrown with romantic vegetation, prompted those interested in architecture to venture farther afield and to explore the Greek mainland and Asia Minor. The first book with detailed illustrations of Greek monuments to be published was the Frenchman Julien-David LeRoy's *Ruines des plus beaux monuments de la Grèce* (1758).

This was followed by *The Antiquities of Athens* by two English architects, James Stuart and Nicholas Revett, which appeared in three parts in 1762, 1789, and 1795. The actual imitation of Greek architecture developed slowly, though the idea of the superiority of Greek over Roman architecture was established by Johann Winckelmann's *Gedanken über die Nachahmung der griechischen Werke in der Malerei und Bildhauerkunst* (1755; *Reflections on the Painting and Sculpture of the Greeks*, 1765).

In this way, Neoclassicism, in its nostalgia for past civilizations and its attempt to re-create order and reason through the adoption of Classical forms, was, paradoxically, also a Romantic movement. Prompted by feeling as well as by reason, architects interested themselves as much in the picturesque aspects of nature and objects in nature (such as ruins) as in rational procedures. The term "Romantic Classicism" has been used by some 20th-century art historians to describe certain aspects of Neoclassical architecture. This term admits non-Greco-Roman forms and the many attempts to imitate Chinese, Moorish, Indian, Egyptian, and, of course, Gothic buildings.

The pursuit of Greek architecture had as one incentive the pursuit of primitive truth and thus of an inherent rationalism. This line of thought had been developed early in the

18th century and was popularized by a French Jesuit, Marc-Antoine Laugier, whose *Essai sur l'architecture* appeared in French in 1753 and in English in 1755. Advocating a return to rationalism and simplicity in building and taking the primitive hut as his example of the fundamental expression of human needs, Laugier was both reacting against the excesses of the Rococo period and laying the theoretical groundwork for Neoclassicism. He did not advocate copying Greek forms, with which he was probably unacquainted, but argued that all forms not having a structural or functional purpose should be eliminated.

The centre of international Neoclassicism was Rome, a gathering place from the 1740s on for talented young artists from all over Europe. Virtually every figure who was to play a significant role in the movement passed through that city. Piranesi arrived in 1740, Anton Raphael Mengs in 1741, Robert Adam in 1754, Winckelmann in 1755, the French painter Jacques-Louis David in 1755, and the Italian sculptor Antonio Canova in 1779. Although it was Rome, the cradle of Italian antiquities, that provided the stage, the leading actors in the Neoclassical drama were French, German, or English; very little was contributed by Italians to this new movement. The centre of activity was the French Academy, where winners of the academy's coveted Prix de Rome went to study the monuments firsthand and to be exposed to the artistic life of the Italian capital. The projects produced by French Prix de Rome winners are characterized by their grandeur of scale; strict geometric organization; simplicity of geometric forms; Greek or Roman detail; dramatic use of columns, particularly to articulate interior spaces and create urban landscapes; and a preference for blank walls and the contrast of formal volumes and textures. The same qualities describe Neoclassical architecture as it was to emerge throughout Europe and in America.

The boldest innovator in the world of French Neoclassical architecture was Claude-Nicolas Ledoux. Like Boullée he designed a number of buildings between 1765 and 1780 in which he attempted to reconcile the traditional elements of French classicism with the new spirit of the antique. Among these were the Château de Bénouville, Calvados (1768–75), and the Hôtel de Montmorency, Paris (c. 1770–72), both of which feature Ionic colonnades with straight entablatures and are somewhat English in feeling. More original were the Pavilion at Louveciennes of 1771 for Madame du Barry, which again invited comparison with contemporary English villas and with the Petit Trianon, and the Hôtel Guimard of 1772. The theatre at Besançon, with its cubic exterior and interior range of baseless columns stylistically derived from those at Paestum, dates from 1775–84.

Both Ireland and Scotland produced significant Neoclassical buildings. In Dublin, James Gandon's Four Courts (1786–1802), with its shallow saucer dome raised on a high columnar drum with echoes of Wren's St. Paul's Cathedral, and his Custom House (1781–91) owe joint allegiance to the Palladianism of Sir William Chambers and contemporary French

The Four Courts building, the home of Ireland's judiciary, stands along the River Liffey in Dublin. Completed in 1802, it is an outstanding example of Neoclassical architecture.

Neoclassicism. Edinburgh, the "Athens of the North," experienced a particularly tenacious Greek Revival. Among its monuments are the Royal High School (begun 1825) by Thomas Hamilton and the Royal Institution (now the Royal Scottish Academy) by William Henry Playfair. David Hamilton built the Royal Exchange (now the Gallery of Modern Art), Glasgow (1829–30), in a style showing the Greek influence, and the revival in that city remained strong well into the 19th century, culminating in the work of Alexander ("Greek") Thomson, whose Caledonia Road Free Church (1856–57) is among the finest monuments of Neoclassical architecture in Scotland.

Neoclassical architecture thrived in the United States throughout the 19th century, and examples of it exist in nearly every major city. The analogy with imperial Rome and later (after the War of Greek Independence, 1821–32, in particular) with the grandeur and political ideals of Periclean Athens strengthened the case for the adoption of Roman and Greek architectural models in the United States. In 1785 Thomas Jefferson planned the Virginia State Capitol with the Frenchman Charles-Louis Clérisseau, taking as his model the ancient Roman Maison-Carrée at Nîmes. It was to be the first public building in the modern world directly based on an antique temple. Jefferson's own house, Monticello, in

Virginia, featured a central-domed space and was indebted to ancient Roman villas as well as to Palladianism and to modern French and English domestic design. If Monticello echoed the private agrarian retreat of Classical statesmen, as described in the writings of Cicero and the younger Pliny, the University of Virginia at Charlottesville (1817–26) was an example of Jefferson's effort to educate the public of the new United States. He conceived the campus as an academic village of extraordinary charm and novelty in which a central Pantheon-like rotunda, containing a library, stands at the head of a grassy open space flanked by two lines of small templelike pavilions, which are linked by colonnades.

PICTURESQUE

An artistic concept and style of the late 18th and early 19th centuries, the picturesque was characterized by a preoccupation with the pictorial values of architecture and landscape in combination with each other. Enthusiasm for the picturesque evolved partly as a reaction against the earlier 18th-century trend of Neoclassicism, with its emphasis on formality, proportion, order, and exactitude. The term "picturesque" originally denoted a landscape scene that looked as if it came out of a painting in the style of

17th-century French artists Claude Lorrain or Gaspard Poussin. In England, the picturesque was defined in a long controversy between landscape designer Sir Uvedale Price and painter Richard Payne Knight as an aesthetic quality existing between the sublime (i.e., awe-inspiring) and the beautiful (i.e., serene), and one marked by pleasing variety, irregularity, asymmetry, and interesting textures. Medieval ruins in a natural landscape, for example, were thought to be quintessentially picturesque.

The picturesque never evolved into a coherent theory, but various works of architecture and landscape gardening display its influence, particularly in an emphasis on the relation between buildings and their natural or landscaped setting. Price was the foremost exponent of the picturesque in landscape gardening. The English architect and town planner John Nash produced some of the most exemplary works incorporating the concept.

The picturesque soon came to include exotic forms from the Near East and the Orient, as well as from Gothic architecture, by then a form of building that had survived only in rural areas. As early as 1750, the English writer Horace Walpole had put Gothic decorations on his villa, Strawberry Hill, just outside London. But the fashion for the medieval historical novel, introduced by Sir Walter Scott, combined with enthusiasm for the picturesque, made the Gothic an alternative style of building by the early 1800s.

GOTHIC REVIVAL

The architectural movement most commonly associated with Romanticism is Gothic Revival, a term first used in England in the mid-19th century to describe buildings being erected in the style of the Middle Ages and later expanded to embrace the entire Neo-Gothic movement. The date of its beginning is not easy to pinpoint, for, even when there was no particular liking for Gothic, conservatism and local building practices had conditioned its use as the style for churches and collegiate buildings. In its earliest phase, therefore, Gothic Revival is not easily distinguished from Gothic survival.

The first clearly self-conscious imitation of Gothic architecture for reasons of nostalgia appeared in England in the early 18th century. Buildings erected at that time in the Gothic manner were for the most part frivolous and decorative garden ornaments, actually more Rococo than Gothic in spirit. But, with the rebuilding beginning in 1747 of the country house Strawberry Hill by Walpole, a new and significant aspect of the revived style was given convincing form, and, by the beginning of the 19th century, picturesque planning and grouping provided the basis for experimentation in architecture. Gothic was especially suited to this aim. Scores of houses with battlements and turrets in the

The home of Horace Walpole, Strawberry Hill House, is one of the earliest examples of Gothic Revival architecture in England. The mansion also inspired the setting of Walpole's most famous novel, *The Castle of Otranto* (1765).

style of a castle were built in England during the last years of the 18th century.

The first architect to study Gothic forms and structure carefully with the aim of accurately reproducing them was the Englishman Augustus Welby Northmore Pugin, who worked in the 1830s and '40s. Pugin, a convert to Roman Catholicism, linked the revival of Gothic

AUGUSTUS WELBY NORTHMORE PUGIN

Augustus Welby Northmore Pugin (b. March 1, 1812, London, England–d. Sept. 14, 1852, London) was the son of the French architect Augustus Charles Pugin, who gave him his architectural and draftsmanship training. A Roman Catholic, the younger Pugin was intent to show that Gothic was an expression of the Catholic spirit and thus the only form of architecture properly suited to its ritual. In his book *Contrasts* (1836) he also sought to show that architecture reflects the state of the society by which it is built: the society of the Middle Ages was good; therefore, Gothic architecture was good. In *The True Principles of Pointed or Christian Architecture* (1841), he first laid down firm principles for the Victorian Gothic Revival. Architecture, he held, should be honest in its expression. Every feature of a building should be essential to its proper functioning and construction, and every feature of this construction should be frankly expressed. Architecture was to be judged by the highest standards of morality. Such concepts are a part of Pugin's French heritage; they were commonplace in 18th-century France, but

(continued on the next page)

(continued from the previous page)

Pugin's ideals came as a revelation to British architects and gave to the Gothic Revival a wholly new seriousness of purpose.

Most of the buildings in which Pugin attempted to give form to his ideas were built between 1837 and 1844. His first church of any consequence was St. Mary's (1837-39), Derby; his most influential were St. Wilfrid's (Hulme, Manchester, 1839-42) and St. Oswald's (Old Swan, Liverpool, 1840-42). But all three—like most of his other buildings and even his own favourite, St. Augustine's (1845-51), built near his house at Ramsgate, Kent—though solid and broadly proportioned and far more convincingly imbued with the Gothic spirit than earlier buildings, are not entirely successful as works of architecture. Pugin was too much concerned with the minutiae of medieval detail. When incomplete in their detail and furnishing, his churches are grim; when fully and expensively finished, as at St. Giles's (Cheadle, Staffordshire, 1841-46) they appear overexquisite.

The death of his second wife in 1844 and the recurrence of an old illness cast a shadow over Pugin's last years. His practice declined as other architects emerged to serve Roman Catholic clients. During his last years he worked with Sir Charles Barry on the new Palace of Westminster.

Pugin's doctrines were taken up by the Anglican reformers, the Tractarians of Oxford and the Camdenians of Cambridge. The Ecclesiological Society, into which the Camden Society was transformed in 1845, so successfully aroused the liturgical enthusiasm of the clergy that most architects employed by the established Church of England in the years that followed were subject to the most doctrinaire of disciplines.

architecture to the revival of religion in society. He espoused the Gothic as a morally correct form of building.

Pugin's ideas were adopted and further developed by the art critic John Ruskin, who contrasted the structural honesty of Gothic architecture with the manipulations and concealments of structure practiced by Renaissance architects. Ruskin's writings, notably *The Seven Lamps of Architecture* (1849) and *The Stones of Venice* (1853) in which he defended truthfulness of structure and richness of ornament in natural forms, were enormously influential. Their effect was reinforced by the writings of the Anglican ecclesiological movement, which inspired Gothic-revival churches in England and America.

These ranged from the extraordinarily expressive and richly decorated church of All Saints, Margaret Street, in London of 1849–59, by William Butterfield, to the modest wood and stone churches designed for rural U.S. sites by Richard Upjohn in the 1840s and '50s. The idea of structural honesty was also extended to secular buildings, resulting in the United States in the simple country villas designed by Andrew Jackson Downing and his followers and culminating in the great houses of the shingle-style movement of the 1870s and '80s and the buildings of Henry Hobson Richardson.

Structural honesty became structural rationalism in the works and writings of the French architect Eugène-Emmanuel Viollet-le-Duc. The most conscientious 19th-century student of Gothic structural techniques, Viollet-le-Duc wrote in favour of the creation of a modern architecture that would use modern materials like iron and glass as rationally as Gothic architecture had used stone. Viollet-le-Duc's writings were widely read in Europe and the United States well into the early 20th century, and they influenced architects as diverse as the Spaniard Antonio Gaudí and the Belgian Victor Horta (both designers in the naturalistic Art Nouveau style) and the American Frank Lloyd Wright, who espoused the organic use of materials.

NEW FORMS

At the same time that the revival of Gothic architecture and the development of new forms based on Gothic structure were taking place, Classicism was continuing to develop in European and American architecture. The monumental Romantic Classicism that appeared about the time of the French Revolution, and its parallel— though more modest—in the new American republic, gradually gave way to more experimental forms.

When Thomas Jefferson designed the University of Virginia at Charlottesville (1817–26), he used Classical forms to evoke the spirit of ancient republics and to teach proper taste to the students. The German architect and painter Karl Friedrich Schinkel put a vast row of columns across the front of his Altes Museum in Berlin (1824–28) in order to produce the sense of grandeur appropriate to a major public building. But even in the work of Schinkel, the Classical style was beginning to be abstracted into a system of post-and-lintel construction that organized space into regular bays.

By the 1830s architects were beginning to question whether the repetition of ancient forms had any meaning for modern society with its new industries, institutions, and standards of living. When Henri Labrouste designed the Bibliothèque Ste-Geneviève in Paris (1838–51), he used the more practical and less imposing arched forms of the Renaissance in a building whose composition and decoration were dictated by its interior organization and purpose rather than by historical model. As the century progressed, architects turned to using the forms of the Classical tradition in more decorative and pictorial ways. In France, Charles Garnier's Paris Opéra (1861–75) reflected the opulence of contemporary society in its baroque forms and rich decorations. It also served as a set piece in the new system of grand boulevards laid out by Baron Georges Eugène Haussmann with the encouragement of the emperor Napoleon III. In the United States the Renaissance and baroque became favoured styles for the houses of wealthy businessmen and for the buildings where they worked and the public institutions they endowed. The firm of McKim, Mead, and White was the best known and most successful architectural servant of the merchant classes, designing such varied works in New York City alone as the Villard houses of 1885 (now part of the New York Palace Hotel), Columbia University of 1893, the University Club of 1900, and Pennsylvania Station of 1906–10 (demolished 1963).

TECHNOLOGY

A dramatic growth in the influence of technology on architecture occurred in the 19th century. With the Industrial Revolution architecture developed a relationship with manufacturing. Industry created a need for new types of buildings, and at the same time new building materials and techniques were being made available by industry. Huge spaces, unobstructed by bulky vertical supports, were needed for factories and mills. The goods they produced were stored in warehouses and shipped from docks and train sheds. When they reached their destinations, they were sold in shops joined by great covered passages or, later in the 19th century, vast department stores. These new buildings were made possible by the development of new technology: first, cast and wrought iron in the late 18th century, and, after the Bessemer process was invented in 1856, steel. Iron and steel are lighter than stone and stronger than wood and can be made quickly into structural elements at a factory and shipped to a construction site.

Iron was frequently combined with glass in the construction of conservatories; early surviving examples include the conservatory (1827–30) at Syon House, Middlesex, by Charles Fowler, and the Palm House (1845–47) at Kew Gardens, Surrey, by Decimus Burton. These led naturally to the Crystal Palace, the climax of early Victorian technology. In the design of the Crystal Palace, built for the Great Exhibition held at London in 1851, Sir Joseph Paxton, a botanist, employed timber, cast iron, wrought iron, and glass in a ridge-and-furrow system he had developed for greenhouses at Chatsworth in 1837. Paxton was partly inspired by the organic structure of the Amazonian lily, *Victoria regia*, which he successfully cultivated. The Crystal Palace contained important innovations in mass production of standardized materials and rapid assembly of parts, but its chief architectural merit lay in its cadence of colossal spaces. French designers recognized its magic, and a series of buildings for universal exhibitions held at Paris in 1855, 1867, and 1878 showed its influence.

The emancipation of markets and stores was no less impressive. Designers erected iron-and-glass umbrellas, such as Victor Baltard's Halles Centrales, Paris (1853–70; demolished 1971). An especially beautiful example of iron-and-glass construction is Henri Labrouste's nine-domed reading room at the Bibliothèque Nationale, Paris (1860–67).

Closer to the English tradition are the billowing Laeken glass houses, Brussels (1868–76), by Alphonse Balat. Visitors were admitted to the Coal Exchange in London (1846–49, J. B. Bunning; demolished 1962) through a round towered Classical porch at the corner of two Renaissance palaces to a magnificent rotunda hall, which was surrounded by three tiers of ornamental iron balconies and roofed by a lacelike dome of iron and glass. In Paris, Gustave Eiffel, together with the architect Louis-Auguste Boileau, gave the retail shop a new and exciting setting in the Bon Marché (1876), where merchandise was displayed around the perimeters of skylighted, interior courts. The United States saw nothing comparable, but cast-iron columns and arches appeared during the 1850s in commercial buildings such as the Harper Brothers Building at New York City (1849) by John B. Corlies and James Bogardus. Stores were given cast-iron faces, as in the pioneering Stewart's Department Store (later Wanamaker's) by John Kellum in New York City (1859–62). Iron was frequently intended to simulate stone, and it was admired for its economy of maintenance as well as such neglected qualities as precision, standardization, and efficient strength. British parallels to these American examples include Gardner's Warehouse (1855–56, Glasgow) by John Baird and Oriel Chambers (1864, Liverpool) by Peter Ellis.

The Eiffel Tower (1887–89), the most important emblem of the Paris exhibition of 1889, was designed by Gustave Eiffel, an engineer who had done outstanding work in the Paris Exposition of 1878 and in steel structures such as the trussed parabolic arches in the viaduct at Garabit, France (1880–84). In the Palais des Machines (at the 1889 exhibition) by Ferdinand Dutert and Victor Contamin, a series of three-hinged trussed arches sprang from small points across a huge space, 385 feet (117 metres) long and 150 feet (45 metres) high. Similar spaces had already been created in railway stations in England such as St. Pancras, London (1864–68, by William H. Barlow), where the wrought-iron arches have a span of 243 feet (74 metres) and rise to a height of 100 feet (30 metres).

It soon became clear that the technology of industrial buildings could be turned to other uses, the most important of which was building more efficiently in the cities where growing population pushed up land values until it became desirable to put tall buildings on small lots. In the booming cities of the United States in the late 19th century, the skyscraper gradually came into being. Little by little, iron and steel supporting elements were added to stone and brick buildings, until in 1885 William LeBaron Jenney designed the Home Insurance Company Building in Chicago, Illinois. It was the first building in which the exterior walls were entirely supported on a steel frame. By the 1890s U.S. cities were dotted with tall office buildings. Architects like Louis Sullivan of Chicago tried to emphasize the simplicity

One of the world's most iconic steel structures, the Eiffel Tower in Paris, France, is exemplary for its metal arches and trusses as well as its lattice-girder piers.

EIFFEL TOWER

The Eiffel Tower is a Parisian landmark that is also a technological masterpiece in building-construction history. When the French government was organizing the International Exposition of 1889 to celebrate the centenary of the French Revolution, a competition was held for designs for a suitable monument. More than 100 plans were submitted, and the Centennial Committee accepted that of the noted bridge engineer Gustave Eiffel. Eiffel's concept of a 984-foot (300-metre) tower built almost entirely of open-lattice wrought iron aroused amazement, skepticism, and no little opposition on aesthetic grounds. When completed, the tower served as the entrance gateway to the exposition.

Nothing remotely like the Eiffel Tower had ever been built; it was twice as high as the dome of St. Peter's in Rome or the Great Pyramid of Giza. In contrast to such older monuments, the tower was erected in only about two years (1887–89), with a small labour force, at slight cost. Making use of his advanced knowledge of the behaviour of metal arch and metal truss forms under loading, Eiffel designed a light, airy, but strong structure that presaged a revolution in civil engineering and architectural design. And, after it opened to the public on May 15, 1889, it ultimately vindicated itself aesthetically.

The Eiffel Tower stands on four lattice-girder piers that taper inward and join to form a single large vertical tower. As they curve inward, the piers are connected to each other by networks of girders at two levels that afford viewing platforms for tourists. By contrast, the four semicircular arches at the tower's base are purely aesthetic elements that serve no structural function. Because of their unique shape, which was dictated partly by engineering considerations but also partly by Eiffel's artistic sense, the piers required elevators to ascend on a curve; the glass-cage machines designed by the Otis Elevator Company of the United States became one of the principal features of the building, helping establish it as one of the world's premier tourist attractions.

The Eiffel tower, with a 17-foot (5-metre) high base and a television antenna at its top, reaches a total elevation of 1,063 feet (324 metres), making it the tallest man-made structure in the world until the Chrysler Building in New York City was topped off with a 180-foot (55-metre) spire in 1929.

and rugged strength of the steel frame in their works but also strove to make them artistic by shaping them or decorating their surfaces. Sullivan, though claiming originality, drew from the geometric and naturalistic ornament of the past, like the Moorish and Gothic, in tall office buildings such as the Wainwright Building in St. Louis (1890–91).

Other architects turned to Classical and medieval forms. The blend of steel construction and stylistic revival produced some of the great U.S. skyscrapers of the early 20th century such as Cass Gilbert's Woolworth Building (1911–13) in New York City and Raymond Hood and John Mead Howells's Tribune Tower (1922–25) in Chicago.

At the very end of the 19th century, the important emblem of modern commerce thus received an appropriate form: its structure

Cass Gilbert's Woolworth Building in New York City, seen here *c.* 1913, was the world's tallest skyscraper until 1930, when the Chrysler Building opened.

was made of steel, its spaces were planned efficiently, its elevations were expressive of the skeleton, and its scale was marked by the fenestration and ornament.

ART NOUVEAU

Although known as Jugendstil in Germany, Sezessionstil in Austria, Modernista in Spain, and Stile Liberty or Stile Floreale in Italy, Art Nouveau has become the general term applied to a highly varied movement that was European-centred but internationally current at the end of the 19th century. Art Nouveau architects gave idiosyncratic expression to many of the themes that had preoccupied the preceding decades, ranging from Viollet-le-Duc's call for structural honesty to Sullivan's call for an organic architecture. The extensive use of iron and glass in Art Nouveau buildings was also rooted in 19th-century practice. In France bizarre forms appeared in iron, masonry, and concrete, such as the structures of Hector Guimard for the Paris Métro (c. 1900), the Montmartre church of Saint-Jean L'Évangéliste (1894–1904) by Anatole de Baudot, Xavier Schollkopf's house for the actress Yvette Guilbert at Paris (1900), and the Samaritaine Department Store (1905) near the Pont Neuf in Paris, by Frantz Jourdain (1847–1935). The Art Nouveau architect's preference for the curvilinear is especially evident in the Brussels buildings of the Belgian Baron Victor Horta. In the Hôtel Van Eetvelde (1895) he used floral, tendrilous ornaments, while his Maison du Peuple (1896–99) exhibits undulating enclosures of space. Decorative exploitation of the architectural surface with flexible, S-shaped linear ornament, commonly called whiplash or eel styles, was indulged in by the Jugendstil and Sezessionstil architects. The Studio Elvira at Munich (1897–98) by August Endell and Otto Wagner's Majolika Haus at Vienna (c. 1898) are two of the more significant examples of this German and Austrian use of line.

Wagner continued to combine academic geometry with Classical modified Art Nouveau decoration in his Karlsplatz Stadtbahn Station (1899–1901) and in the Postal Savings Bank (1904–06), both in Vienna. Wagner's pupils broke free of his classicism and, along with a group of Austrian artists, formed the Vienna Sezession in 1897. Joseph Olbrich joined the art colony at Darmstadt, Germany, where his houses and exhibition gallery of about 1905 were boxlike, severe buildings. Josef Hoffmann left Wagner to found the Wiener Werkstätte, an Austrian equivalent of the English Arts and Crafts Movement; his best work, the Stoclet House at Brussels (1905; designated a UNESCO World Heritage site, 2009), was an asymmetrical composition in which white planes were defined at the edges by gilt lines and decorated by formalized Art Nouveau motifs reminiscent of Wagner's ornament. Josef

Plecnik, a talented pupil of Wagner, began his career in 1903–05 with the office and residence of Johannes Zacherl in Vienna. This was in a Wagner-inspired style that Plecnik developed in the 1930s in a fascinating series of buildings, especially in his native city of Ljubljana, now in Slovenia.

In Finland, Eliel Saarinen brought an Art Nouveau flavour to the National Romanticism current in the years around 1900. His Helsinki Railway Station (1906–14) is close to the work of Olbrich and the Viennese Sezessionists. Close links existed between Art Nouveau designers in Vienna and in Glasgow, where Charles Rennie Mackintosh's School of Art (1896–1909), with its rationalist yet poetic aesthetic, is one of the most inventive and personal of all Art Nouveau buildings. In the Netherlands, Hendrik Petrus Berlage also created a sternly fundamentalist language of marked individuality that is best appreciated in his masterpiece, the Amsterdam Exchange (1898–1903). The exterior is in a rugged and deliberately unpicturesque vernacular, while the even more ruthless interior deploys brick, iron, and glass in a manner that owes much to the rationalist aesthetic of Viollet-le-Duc.

In the United States the Art Nouveau movement arrived with designer Louis Comfort Tiffany and was especially influential on ornamental rather than spatial design, particularly on Sullivan's decorative schemes and, for a

This detail of the front facade of Casa Batlló (1904–06) by Antoni Gaudí exemplifies the architect's signature use of colour, texture, and freedom of form.

time, those of Frank Lloyd Wright. Similarly, in Italy decorative exuberance and the formally picturesque were elements of Stile Floreale buildings by Raimondo D'Aronco, such as the main building for the Applied Art Exhibition held at Turin, Italy, in 1902. These qualities, along with dynamic spatial innovations, were manifested in the works of perhaps the most singular Art Nouveau architect, the Spaniard Antoni Gaudí. His imaginative and dramatic experiments with space, form, structure, and ornament fascinate the visitor to Barcelona. With their peculiar organicism, the Casa Milá apartment house (1905–10), the residence of the Batlló family (1904–06), Gaudí's unfinished lifetime projects of the surrealistic Güell Park and the enigmatic church of the Holy Family were personal statements. Their effect, like that of most Art Nouveau architecture, was gained through bizarre form and ornament.

CHAPTER SEVEN

ARCHITECTURE IN THE 20TH AND 21ST CENTURIES

American technical and stylistic innovations of the early 20th century were quickly recognized in Europe. Not only the skyscrapers but also the houses of Chicago architect Frank Lloyd Wright were widely written about and admired. The abstract, floating planes of the exterior of a building like the Robie House of 1909 in Chicago were seen by Europeans as an escape from historical forms. After the crisis of World War I and the political changes of that period, architects in France, Germany, and Russia started looking for ways to create a new architecture that did not use past styles.

THE MODERNIST MOVEMENT

The Modernist movement in architecture was an attempt to create a nonhistorical architecture of Functionalism in which a new sense of space would be created with the help of modern materials. A reaction against the stylistic pluralism of the 19th century, Modernism was also coloured by the belief that the 20th century had given birth to "modern man," who would need a radically new kind of architecture.

EUROPE

The Viennese architect Adolf Loos opposed the use of any ornament at all and designed purist compositions of bald, functional blocks such as the Steiner House at Vienna (1910), one of the first private houses of reinforced concrete. Peter Behrens, having had contact with Joseph Olbrich at Darmstadt and with Josef Hoffmann at Vienna, was in 1907 appointed artistic adviser in charge of the German electrical equipment company Allgemeine Elektricitäts Gesellschaft (AEG), for which he designed a turbine factory (1909) at Berlin. Behrens strongly affected three great architects who worked in his office: Walter Gropius, Le Corbusier, and Ludwig Mies van der Rohe.

In Germany, Gropius followed a mechanistic direction. His Fagus Works factory at Alfeld-an-der-Leine in Germany (1911) and the Werkbund exposition building at the Cologne exhibition (1914) had been models of industrial architecture in which vigorous forms were enclosed by masonry and glass; the effect of these buildings was gained by the use of steel frames, strong silhouette, and the logic of their plans. There were no historical influences or expressions of local landscape, traditions, or materials. The beauty of the buildings derived from adapting form to a technological culture.

Gropius became director of the ducal Arts and Crafts School at Weimar in 1919. Later called the Bauhaus, it became the most important centre of modern design until the Nazis closed it in 1933. While he was at Weimar, Gropius developed a firm philosophy about architecture and education, which he announced in 1923. The aim of the visual arts, he said, is to create a complete, homogeneous physical environment in which all the arts have their place. Architects, sculptors, furniture makers, and painters must learn practical crafts and obtain knowledge of tools, materials, and forms; they must become acquainted with the machine and attempt to use it in solving the social problems of an industrial society. At the Bauhaus, aesthetic investigations into space, colour, construction, and elementary forms were flavoured by Cubism and Constructivism. Moving the school to Dessau in 1925, Gropius designed the pioneering new Bauhaus (1925–26) in which steel frames and glass walls provided workshops within severely Cubistic buildings.

The Bauhaus art school, itself a remarkable example of Modernist architecture designed by Walter Gropius, turned out numerous influential artists, designers, and architects until its closing in 1933.

Gropius assembled a staff of Modernist teachers, including the artists László Moholy-Nagy, Wassily Kandinsky, and Paul Klee, designer Marcel Breuer, and architect Adolf Meyer, whose projects, such as the 116 experimental standardized housing units of the Törten Estate at Dessau, Germany (1926–28), bore a highly machinized, depersonalized appearance.

In France, Tony Garnier caught the Modernist currents in materials, structure, and composition when he evolved his masterful plan for a *Cité industrielle* (1901–04), published in 1917, in which reinforced concrete was to be used to create a modern city of modern buildings. With insight, Garnier developed a comprehensive scheme for residential neighbourhoods, transportation terminals, schools, and industrial centres, and his plan became a major influential scheme for 20th-century urban design. Garnier received no mandate to build such a city, but his town hall at Boulogne-Billancourt (1931–34) recalled the promise he had shown, though it was not as innovative and masterful as might have been expected.

A member of the Futurist movement and influenced by American industrial cities and the Viennese architects Otto Wagner and Adolf Loos, Italian architect Antonio Sant'Ella designed a grandiose futuristic city, entitled "Città nuova" ("New City"), the drawings for which were exhibited at Milan in 1914. He conceived of the city as a symbol of the new technological age. It was an affirmative environment for the future, however, in opposition to the negating inhuman Expressionistic city of the future conceived by Fritz Lang in the 1926 film classic *Metropolis*.

Centred in Germany between 1910 and 1925, Expressionist architects, such as the painters who were part of the Brücke ("Bridge") and Blaue Reiter ("Blue Rider") groups, sought peculiarly personal and often bizarre visual forms and effects. Among the earliest manifestations of an Expressionistic building style were the highly individual early works of Hans Poelzig, such as the Luban Chemical Factory (1911–12) and the municipal water tower (1911) of Posen, Germany (now Poznań, Poland), which led to his monumental, visionary "space caves," such as the project for the Salzburg Festival Theatre (1920–21) and the Grosses Schauspielhaus, built in Berlin (1919) for Max Reinhardt's Expressionistic theatre. These later works by Poelzig show the influence of the structural audacity of Max Berg's Centenary Hall in Breslau, Germany (now Wrocław, Poland; 1912–13), with its gigantic reinforced concrete dome measuring 213 feet (65 metres) in diameter. The second generation of Expressionists centred their activities in postwar Germany and the Netherlands. Distinctly personal architectural statements were given form in such dynamically sculptured structures as the Einstein Observatory in Potsdam (1920), by Erich Mendelsohn; the anthroposophically based design by Rudolf Steiner for the Goetheanum in Dornach, Switzerland (1925–28); the Eigen Haard Estates (housing development) at Amsterdam (1921), by Michel de Klerk; and Fritz Höger's Chilehaus office building in Hamburg (1922–23), with its imperative thrust of mass and acute angularity.

As Germany was the centre of Expression-
ism, Paris was the stronghold of the advocates
of a new vision of space: Cubism, developed
by Georges Braque and Pablo Picasso about
1906. Forms were dismembered into their
faceted components; angular forms, interpen-
etrated planes, transparencies, and diverse
impressions were recorded as though seen
simultaneously. Soon architectural reflections
of the Cubist aesthetic appeared internationally. Interior spaces were defined by thin,
discontinuous planes and glass walls; supports were reduced to slender metal columns,
machine-finished and without ornamentation;
and Cubistic voids and masses were arranged
programmatically in asymmetric compositions.

The Dutch De Stijl movement was influenced by Cubism, although it sought a
greater abstract purity in its geometric formalism. Organized in Leiden in 1917, the painters
Piet Mondrian and Theo van Doesburg and
the architects Jacobus Johannes Pieter Oud
and Gerrit Thomas Rietveld were counted
among its members. Their "Neoplastic" aesthetic advocated severe precision of line and
shape, austerely pristine surfaces, a Spartan
economy of form, and purity of colour. Rietveld's Schroeder House, built in 1924 in Utrecht,
was a three-dimensional parallel to Mondrian's paintings of the period. Van Doesburg's
work for the Bauhaus art school at Weimar
brought the influence of Dutch Neoplasticism

to bear upon Gropius and Mies, whose plans for houses at times markedly resembled van Doesburg's paintings. Meanwhile Oud collaborated with van Doesburg for a time and vigorously proclaimed the new style in housing developments he built in Rotterdam (after 1918), Hook of Holland (1924–27), and Stuttgart, Germany (1927).

Cubism and the related movements of Futurism, Constructivism, Suprematism, and Neoplasticism, like any artistic styles, might have faltered and fallen into a merely decorative cliché, as at the Paris Exposition of 1925, but for Gropius, Mies van der Rohe, and Le Corbusier.

Gropius was succeeded at the Bauhaus in 1930 by Mies van der Rohe, whose training as a mason was supplemented by the engineering experience he had gained from 1908 to 1911 in the office of Behrens; both of these elements of his education were synthesized in his project for the Kröller House in The Hague (1912). Influenced by van Doesburg's De Stijl, Mie's natural elegance and precise orderliness soon revealed themselves in unrealized projects for a brick country house, a steel-and-glass skyscraper, and a glazed, cantilevered concrete-slab office building (1920–22). He directed the Weissenhof estate project of the Werkbund Exposition in Stuttgart (1927), contributing the design for an apartment house. Such practical problems failed to show his talent, which was not fully known until he designed the German pavilion for the International Exposition at Barcelona in 1929. The continuous spaces partitioned with thin marble planes and the chromed steel columns drew international applause. His Tugendhat House in Brno, Czech Republic (1930), along with Le Corbusier's Villa Savoye, epitomized the Modernist domestic setting at its best.

The Swiss-French architect Charles-Édouard Jeanneret, known as Le Corbusier, gave the new architecture, sometimes referred to as the International Style, a firm foundation by writing the strong theoretical statement, *Vers une architecture* (*Towards a New Architecture*), published in 1923. It revealed a world of new forms—not Classical capitals and Gothic arches but ships, turbines, grain elevators, airplanes, and machine products, which Le Corbusier said were indexes to 20th-century imagination. His love of machines was combined with a belief in communal authority as the best means of accomplishing social reforms, and Le Corbusier directed his attention toward the problems of housing and urban patterns. An architectural attack, using standardized building components and mass production, was required. His sociological and formal ideas appeared in a Cubist project for "Dom-Ino" housing (1914), and his aesthetic preferences led him to develop an extreme version of Cubist painting that he and

the painter Amédée Ozenfant called Purism.
Returning to architecture in 1921, he designed
a villa in Vaucresson, France (1922), the
abstract planes and strip windows of which
revealed his desire to "arrive at the house
machine"—that is, standardized houses with
standardized furniture. In 1922 he also brought
forth his project for a skyscraper city of 3 million people, in which tall office and apartment
buildings would stand in broad open plazas
and parks with the Cubist spaces between
them defined by low row housing.

Much of his work thereafter—his Voisin
city plan, his Pavilion of the New Spirit at the
Paris Exposition of 1925, his exhibit of workers'
apartments at the Werkbund Exposition
in Stuttgart (1927), and his influential but
unexecuted submittal to the League of
Nations competition—was a footnote to that
dream of a new city. The villa, Les Terrasses,
at Garches, France (1927), was a lively play
of spatial parallelepipeds (six-sided solid
geometric forms the faces of which are par-
allelograms) ruled by horizontal planes, but
his style seemed to culminate in the most
famous of his houses, the Villa Savoye in
Poissy, France (1929–31). The building's principal block was raised one story above the
ground on pilotis (heavy reinforced-concrete
columns); floors were cantilevered to permit
long strip windows; and space was molded
plastically and made to flow horizontally,

vertically, and diagonally until, on the top-most terrace, the whole composition ended in a cadenza of rounded, terminating spaces. Gaining greater facility in manipulating flowing spaces, Le Corbusier designed the dormitory for Swiss students at the Cité Universitaire (1931–32) in Paris.

In the period after the Russian Revolution of 1917, the erstwhile Soviet Union at first encouraged modern art, and several architects, notably the German Bruno Taut, looked to the new government for a sociological program. "The Monument to the Third International," (1920) by Vladimir Tatlin, was one of the first buildings conceived entirely in abstract terms. A striking, machine-like design, it consisted of a leaning spiral iron framework supporting a glass cylinder, a glass cone, and a glass cube, each of which could be rotated at different speeds. It was never built owing to the Soviet government's disapproval of nonfigurative art. A workers' club in Moscow (1929) had a plan resembling half a gear, and the Ministry of Central Economic Planning (1928–32), designed by Le Corbusier, was intended to be a glass-filled slab but, because of Stalin's dislike of modern architecture, was never completed. Its foundation later was used for an outdoor swimming pool.

Modern European styles of architecture were subjected to official disfavour in the Soviet Union in the 1930s, as Stalin's government adopted Classical monuments—such as Boris Mikhaylovich Iofan's winning design for the Palace of the Soviets (1931), which was intended to pile Classical colonnades to a height of 1,365 feet (416 metres) and have a colossal statue of Lenin at its summit. With its gigantic Corinthian columns, the building for the Central Committee of the Communist Party in Kiev (1937) showed an overbearing scale.

After 1930 the Modernist movement spread through Europe. In Switzerland Robert Maillart's experiments with reinforced concrete attained great grace in his Salginatobel Bridge (1930). Finland's Alvar Aalto won a competition for the Municipal Library at Viipuri (now Vyborg, Russia) in 1927 with a building of glass walls, flat roof, and round skylights (completed 1935; destroyed 1943); but he retained the traditional Scandinavian sympathy for wood and picturesque planning that were evident in his Villa Mairea at Noormarkku, Finland (1938–39), the factory and housing at Sunila, Kotka, Finland (1936–39, completed 1951–54), and his later civic centre at Säynätsalo, Finland (1950–52). Aalto and other Scandinavians gained a following among those repelled by severe German Modernism. Sweden's Gunnar Asplund and Denmark's Kay Fisker, Christian Frederick Møller, and Arne Jacobsen also brought regional character into their Modernist work. In the Netherlands, Johannes Andreas Brinkman and Lodewijk Cornelis van der Vlugt aimed at more mechanistic, universal form in the Van Nelle Tobacco Factory in Rotterdam (1928–30). In England, refugees from Germany and other countries, alone or with English designers, inaugurated a radical Modernism—for example, the apartment block known as Highpoint I, Highgate, London (by Berthold Lubetkin and the Tecton group, 1935).

THE UNITED STATES

The locus for creative architecture in the United States remained the Midwest, although Californians such as the brothers Charles Sumner Greene and Henry Mather Greene struck occasional regional and modern notes, as in the Gamble House at Pasadena, California (1908–09). The second generation of architects of the Chicago School, such as William G. Purcell, George Grant Elmslie, and William Drummond, disseminated Midwestern modern architecture throughout the United States.

The greatest of all these new Chicago architects was Frank Lloyd Wright. His "prairie architecture" expressed its site, region, structure, and materials and avoided all historical reminiscences; beginning with its plan and a distinctive spatial theme, each building burgeoned to its exterior sculptural form. Starting from Henry Hobson Richardson's rustic, shingle houses and making free use of Beaux-Arts composition during the 1880s and 1890s,

Wright hinted at his prairie house idiom with
the Winslow House in River Forest, Illinois (1893),
elaborated it in the Coonley House in Riverside,
Illinois (1908), and, ultimately, realized it in the
flowing volumes of space defined by sculptural masses and horizontal planes of his Robie
House in Chicago (completed 1909). Meanwhile, he scored a triumph with his administration building for the Larkin Company in Buffalo,
New York, in 1904 (destroyed 1950), which
grouped offices around a central skylighted
court, sealed them hermetically against their
smoky environs, and offered amenities in cir-
culation, air conditioning, fire protection, and
plumbing. In its blocky fire towers, sequences
of piers and recessed spandrels were coupled
together in a powerful composition. Wright
was, however, ignored by all except a select
following. The buildings of the single figure who
gave international distinction to early 20th-cen-
tury American architecture remained the
cherished property of personal clients, such as
Aline Barnsdall, for whom Wright designed the
Hollyhock House in Los Angeles (1918–20).

Wright's autobiography (1943) recorded
his frustrations in gaining acceptance for
organic architecture. The first edition summa-
rized the chief features of that architecture:
the reduction to a minimum in the number
of rooms and the definition of them by point
supports; the close association of buildings to
their sites by means of extended and empha-

FRANK LLOYD WRIGHT

Considered the most influential architect of his time, Frank Lloyd Wright (b. June 8, 1867, Richland Center, Wisconsin, United States–d. April 9, 1959, Phoenix, Arizona) designed about 1,000 structures. He described his "organic architecture" as one that "proceeds, persists, creates, according to the nature of man and his circumstances as they both change." As a pioneer whose ideas were well ahead of his time, Wright had to fight for acceptance of every new design.

Wright's early influences were his clergyman father's playing of Bach and Beethoven and his mother's teaching according to the kindergarten method of Friedrich Froebel. He entered the University of Wisconsin at 15 as a special student, studying engineering because the school had no course in architecture.

Wright left Madison in 1887 to work as a draftsman in Chicago. The next year he joined the firm of Adler and Sullivan, soon becoming Louis Sullivan's chief assistant. Wright was tasked with most of the firm's house designing, and to pay his many debts he designed for private clients in his spare time. Sullivan disapproved, and Wright set up his own office.

As an independent architect, Wright became the leader of a style known as the Prairie school. Houses with low-pitched roofs and extended lines that blend into the landscape typify the style. In 1904 he designed the strong, functional Larkin Building in Buffalo, New York, and in 1906 the Unity Temple in Oak Park, Illinois. In 1911 he returned to build a house on his grandfather's Wisconsin farm, Taliesin (Welsh for "shining brow"). In 1916 he designed the Imperial Hotel in Tokyo, floating the structure on an underlying sea of mud; this resulted in little damage being done to the building in the catastrophic earthquake of 1923.

When the depression of the 1930s limited new construction, Wright wrote and lectured widely. In 1932 he established the Taliesin Fellowship. In this school students learned by working with building materials and with problems of design and construction. From 1938 the school moved in winter from Wisconsin to Taliesin West, a desert camp near Phoenix, Arizona.

In the mid-1930s Wright began an exceptional burst of creative activity. Some of his most famous works date from the period: Fallingwater, a luxurious weekend house in Pennsylvania; the S.C. Johnson &

(continued on the next page)

(continued from the previous page)

Son Administration Building in Racine, Wisconsin (a research tower was added ten years later); and the first Jacobs house in Madison, Wisconsin, the start of a series of ingenious do-it-yourself houses Wright called Usonian.

Except during World War II, Wright continued to build. Notable late works included more houses as well as the Unitarian Church, Shorewood Hills, Wisconsin (1948); the Price Tower, Bartlesville, Oklahoma (1952); Beth Sholom Synagogue, Elkins Park, Pennsylvania (1954); Annunciation Greek Catholic Church, Milwaukee, Wisconsin (1956); the Solomon R. Guggenheim Museum, New York City (1956); and the Marin County Civic Center, San Raphael, California (1957–66).

Although Wright's work was always controversial, he was recognized in Europe as early as 1910 with the publication in Germany of his drawings. In 1925 the Dutch architectural magazine *Wendingen* produced a book of his life's work, and *Architectural Forum* devoted entire issues to his work in 1938 and 1949. He was awarded the gold medal of the Royal Institute of British Architects in 1941, but it was not until 1949 that he received a similar medal from the American Institute of Architects.

Wright lived a flamboyant life that was filled with personal tragedy and constant financial difficulty. He married three times and had seven children. His autobiography first appeared in 1932 and was expanded and reprinted in 1943.

sized planes parallel to the ground; the free flow of space, unencumbered by boxlike enclosures; harmony of all openings with each other and with human scale; the exploitation of the nature of a material, in both its surface manifestations and its structure; the incorporation of mechanical equipment and furniture as organic parts of structure; and the elimination of applied decoration. There were also four new properties: transparency, which was obtained through the use of glass; tenuity, or plasticity of mass achieved through the use of steel in tension, as in reinforced concrete; naturalism, or the expression of materials; and integration, in which all ornamental features were natural by-products of manufacture and assembly.

His Millard House in Pasadena, California (1923), exemplified many of these principles; its concrete-block walls were cast with decorative patterns. Taliesin East, Wright's house near Spring Green, Wisconsin, went through a series of major rebuildings (1911, 1914, 1915, and 1925), and each fitted the site beautifully; local stone, gabled roofs, and outdoor gardens reflected the themes of the countryside. A period of withdrawal at Taliesin afforded Wright several years of intensive reflection, from which he emerged with fabulous drawings for the Doheny ranch in California (1921), a skyscraper for the National Life Insurance Company at Chicago (1920–25), and St. Mark's Tower, New York City (1929). The last was to have been an 18-story apartment house comprising a concrete stem from which four arms branched outward to form the sidewalls of apartments cantilevered from the stem to an exterior glass wall. Unexecuted like most of Wright's most exciting projects, St. Mark's Tower testified to his revolutionary thinking about skyscraper architecture. His ideas gained a wide hearing in 1931 when he published the Kahn lectures he had delivered at Princeton in 1930. In keeping with the needs of the United States during the Great Depression, Wright turned his attention to the low-cost house, designing a "Usonian house" for Herbert Jacobs near Madison, Wisconsin (1937), and a quadruple house, "the Sun houses," at Ardmore, Pennsylvania (1939). These exemplified the residences he intended for his ideal communities, such as rural, decentralized Broadacre City (1936), which was Wright's answer to European schemes for skyscraper cities.

Cantilevered over a waterfall, Frank Lloyd Wright's masterpiece Fallingwater in Mill Run, Pennsylvania, was a country retreat that is now open to visitors.

At about the same time, Wright produced four masterpieces: Fallingwater in Bear Run, Pennsylvania (1936), the daringly cantilevered weekend house of Edgar Kaufmann; the administration building of S.C. Johnson & Son in Racine, Wisconsin, in which brick cylinders and planes develop a series of echoing spaces, culminating in the forest of graceful "mushroom" columns in the main hall; the Johnson House (1937), aptly called Wingspread, also at Racine; and Taliesin West at Paradise Valley, near Phoenix, Arizona (begun 1938), where rough, angular walls and roofs echo the desert valley and surrounding mountains. With increasing sensitivity to local terrain and native forms and materials, Wright stated more complex spatial and structural themes than European Modernists, who seldom attempted either extreme programmatic plans or organic adaptation of form to a particular environment. Eventually, Wright himself developed a more universal geometry, as he revealed in the sculptural Solomon R. Guggenheim Museum in New York City (1956–59).

During the period, some buildings gained attention through their Classical ornament; others were Renaissance palaces. The emblem of business, the office building, sometimes suffered from the demand for unique, distinctive towers; indeed, Harvey Wiley Corbett, a New York architect, admitted that publicity was the ruling motivation for some designers. The

Gothic skyscraper, popularized by Gilbert's Woolworth Building, was the style used by Raymond M. Hood for his winning entry in the *Chicago Tribune* competition (1922), beating out many seemingly more contemporary, albeit less splashy, entries.

About 1920 some architects developed simple cubical forms, and the stepped ziggurat was popularized by renderers, notably Hugh Ferriss. This soaring and jagged form received legal support from the New York City zoning law of 1916 and economic justification from the fact that, in order to obtain rentable, peripheral office space in the upper floors, where the banks of elevators diminished, whole increments of office space had to be omitted. These cubical envelopes were not without ornament at their crests, as in Hood's American Radiator Building in New York City (1924–25), suitably described as "one huge cinder incandescent at the top." Such decoration might be chic, as in New York City's Barclay–Vesey (telephone company) Building, where Ralph Walker re-created the Art Deco interiors of the Paris Exposition of 1925. In San Francisco, Miller, Pflueger, & Cantin used Chinese ornament to enliven their telephone building (1926). Paradoxically, one archaeological find led to simpler buildings when, about 1930, Mayan pyramids inspired Timothy Pflueger in his work on the 450 Sutter building in San Francisco. Clifflike blocks arose in Chicago, the Daily News and Palmolive buildings (1929) being the best examples; New York City acquired a straightforward expression of tall vertical piers and setback cubical masses in the Daily News Building (1930), by the versatile Hood, who had run the course from Gothic to modern form. The bank and office building of the Philadelphia Savings Fund Society (1931–32) by George Howe and William Lescaze, a Swiss architect, gave the skyscraper its first thoroughly 20th-century form, and Hood, again, produced a counterpart in New York City, the McGraw-Hill Building (1931). Few of these, including the Empire State Building (1931), did anything to solve urban density and transportation problems; indeed, they intensified them. Rockefeller Center, however, begun in 1929, was, with its space for pedestrians within a complex of slablike skyscrapers, outstanding and too seldom copied.

American industry showed some inclination to respect function, materials, and engineering between the world wars, as was evident in Joseph Leland's glazed, skeletal buildings for the Pressed Steel Company at Worcester, Massachusetts (1930). Occasionally, a traditional architect had produced an innovation, such as Willis Polk's Hallidie Building at San Francisco (1918). With the aid of Ernest Wilby, the engineering firm of Albert Kahn created a work of architectural merit in Detroit's Continental Motors Factory (about 1918). The National Cash Register, United States Shoe Company, National Biscuit, Sears, Roebuck and Company, and various automobile companies, such as Ford, sponsored Functional architecture.

Rockefeller Center was proof that by 1930 there was a move toward simple form, which was presaged by the architecture of the TVA (Tennessee Valley Authority). European Modernism gained a firm following in the United States as some of its best practitioners emigrated there. Eliel Saarinen, who won second prize in the *Chicago Tribune* competition, gained the acclaim of Sullivan and other architects. He settled in Bloomfield Hills, Michigan, a Detroit suburb, where he established a school of architecture at the Cranbrook Academy of Art. Saarinen designed its new buildings, gradually freeing himself from historical reminiscences of his native Scandinavia. He remained sensitive to the role of art in architecture, best revealed by his use of the sculpture of the Swede Carl Milles. The Austrian architect Richard Neutra established a practice in California, notable products of which were the Lovell House at Los Angeles (1927–28) and the Kaufmann Desert House at Palm Springs (1946–47).

A modern architecture exhibit at the Museum of Modern Art, New York City, in 1932, recorded by the architectural historian Henry-Russell Hitchcock and the architect Philip Johnson in the book *International Style: Architecture Since 1922*, familiarized Americans with the International Style. After 1933, as Modernists fled the Soviet Union, Germany, and Italy, the United States received Gropius, Breuer, and Mies. Gropius joined the architectural school of Harvard University and established an educational focus recalling the Bauhaus.

AFTER WORLD WAR II

Initially, the leading interwar architects of Modernism, Gropius, Mies van der Rohe, Le Corbusier, Wright, and Aalto, continued to dominate the scene. In the United States, Gropius, with Breuer, introduced modern houses to Lincoln, Massachusetts, a Boston suburb, and formed a group, the Architects Collaborative, the members of which designed the thoroughly modern Harvard Graduate Center (1949–50). Mies became dean of the department of architecture at the Illinois Institute of Technology at Chicago in 1938 and designed its new campus. Crown Hall (1952–56) marked the apogee of this quarter-century project.

Beginning with private houses by Hood, Lescaze, Edward Stone, Neutra, Gropius, and Breuer during the 1930s, American Modernism gradually supplanted the historical styles in a range of building types, including schools and churches; for example, Eliel Saarinen's simple, brick Christ Lutheran Church (1949–50) in Minneapolis, Minnesota.

After World War II, big industry turned to
modern architects for distinctive emblems of
prestige. The Connecticut General Life Insurance
Company hired one of the largest modern firms,
Skidmore, Owings & Merrill, to design their new
decentralized headquarters outside Hartford,
Connecticut (1955–57). Lever Brothers turned
to the same firm for New York City's Lever House
(1952), in which the parklike plaza, glass-
curtain walls, and thin aluminum mullions realized the dreams of Mies and others in the 1920s
of freestanding crystalline shafts. Designed by
Eliel Saarinen's son Eero, the General Motors
Technical Center (1948–56) in Warren, Michigan,
was compared with Versailles in its extent, grandeur, and rigorous conformity to an austere,
geometric aesthetic of Miesian forms. The Har-
rison and Abramovitz's tower for the Aluminum
Company of America at Pittsburgh (1954)
advertised its own product, as did Skidmore,
Owings & Merrill's Inland Steel Building in Chicago (1955–57). Perhaps the most chaste of
all was the Seagram Building (1954–58) in New
York City, designed by Mies and Philip Johnson.
Wright alone avoided the rectilinear geometry
of these office buildings. In 1955 he saw his Price
Tower rise at Bartlesville, Oklahoma, a richly faceted, concrete and copper fulfillment of the St.
Mark's Tower he had designed more than 25
years earlier.

About 1952 there was a significant shift
within Modernism from what had come to be

called Functionalism, or the International Style, toward a monumental formalism. There was increasing interest in highly sculptural masses and spaces, as well as in the decorative qualities of diverse building materials and exposed structural systems. Wright's Guggenheim Museum is a manifestation of this aesthetic. Those who had focused their attention on the rectilinear portions of Le Corbusier's Savoye House and Unité d'Habitation apartments at Marseille (1946–52), tended to ignore the plastic sculpture on the roofs of those buildings; to such people, Le Corbusier's highly individual buildings at Chandigarh, India (begun 1950), and the cavernous space in the lyrical church of Notre-Dame-du-Haut (1950–55) at Ronchamp, France, seemed to be examples of personal whimsy. Pier Luigi Nervi in Italy gave structural integrity to the complex curves and geometry of reinforced-concrete structures, such as the Orbetello aircraft hangar (begun 1938) and Turin's exposition hall (1948–50). The Spaniard Eduardo Torroja, his pupil Felix Candela, and the American Frederick Severud followed his lead. Essentially, each attempted to create an umbrella roof the interior space of which could be subdivided as required, such as Torroja's grandstand for the Zarzuela racetrack in Madrid (1935). Mies constructed rectilinear versions of such a space in Crown Hall and in his Farnsworth House at Plano, Illinois (1946–50), while Philip Johnson allowed a single functional unit, the brick-cylinder utility stack, to protrude from his precise glass house at New Canaan, Connecticut (1949). Other designers used curvilinear structural geometry, best indicated by Matthew Nowicki's sports arena at Raleigh, North Carolina (1952–53), in which two tilted parabolic arches, supported by columns, and a stretched-skin roof enclose a colossal space devoid of interior supports. In 1949 Nowicki had challenged Louis Sullivan's precept, form follows function, with another, form follows form; this dictum helped free architecture from programmatic expression. Hugh Stubbins's congress hall in Berlin (1957) and Eero Saarinen's Trans World Airlines terminal at John F. Kennedy International Airport, New York City (1956–62), were outstanding examples of these dynamically monumental, single-form buildings the geometric shapes and silhouettes of which were derived from mathematical computation and technological innovation. International competitions for the opera house in Sydney (1957) and a government centre in Toronto (1958) were won by the Dane Jørn Utzon and the Finn Viljo Revell, respectively. Both architects were exponents of the new monumentalism.

These designs posed problems in structural engineering and in scale, but many architects, such as the American Minoru Yamasaki in the McGregor Building for Wayne State University in Detroit (1958), attempted to make structure become decorative, while the decorative screen, as used by Edward Durell Stone at the United States embassy in New Delhi (1957–59), offered a device for wrapping programmatic interiors within a rich pattern of sculptured walls.

In the United States, after 1959, office buildings for administrative headquarters of large corporations followed the 1955–57 suburban-campus model of Skidmore, Owings & Merrill's Connecticut General Life Insurance Company or, if urban, the towerlike form, often with strong structural expression (e.g., Torre Velasca, Milan, by Belgiojoso, Peressutti, and Rogers, 1959) or the slab form, usually emphasizing glazed walls (e.g., Mannesmann Building, Düsseldorf, Germany, by Paul Schneider-Esleben, 1959), but they rarely achieved an urban composition such as the 1962 Place Ville-Marie, built in Montreal by the Chinese-born American architect I.M. Pei.

Air transportation, trade exhibitions, and spectator sports summoned the often awesome spatial resources of modern technology. Rome's Pallazzi dello Sport done by Nervi (1960), Eero Saarinen's Dulles International Airport, Chantilly, Virginia (1958–62), and Chicago's exposition hall, McCormick Place, by C.F. Murphy and Associates (1971), are examples of the colossal spaces achieved at the time in reinforced concrete or steel and glass. International exhibitions seldom offered comparable architecture. At the New York World's Fair (1964) the Spanish pavilion by Javier Carvajal was a building of merit. There were also several notable examples at Montreal's Expo 67: the West German pavilion by Frei Otto, the United States pavilion by R. Buckminster Fuller, and the startling Constructivist apartment house, Habitat 67, by the Israeli Moshe Safdie, in association with David, Barott, and Boulva, whose 158 precast-concrete apartment units were hoisted into place and post-tensioned to permit dramatic cantilevers and terraces. World's fairs continued to provide a setting for occasionally distinguished examples of modern structures that demonstrated innovations in building technology.

Much significant architecture in the postwar period was sponsored by cultural centres and educational institutions, such as Berlin's philharmonic hall (1963) by Hans Scharoun. Louis I. Kahn, in his design for the Richards Medical Research Building (1960), gave the University of Pennsylvania in Philadelphia a linear programmatic composition of laboratories, each served by vertical systems for circulating gases, liquids, and electricity. Paul Rudolph's art and architecture building (1963) at Yale University in New Haven, Connecticut, gathered its studios, galleries, classrooms, and light wells on 36 interpenetrating levels distributed over six stories. The Morse and Stiles colleges (1962), also at Yale, were designed by Eero Saarinen and set a new standard for multiple-entry urban dormitories. Even the traditionalist campuses of New England preparatory schools gained modern architecture, such as the art building and science building at Phillips Academy in Andover, Massachusetts, by Benjamin A. Thomson (1963) and the dormitories at St. Paul's School in Concord, New Hampshire, by Edward Larrabee Barnes (1965).

The innovations in educational architecture were international. In England, distinctive educational architecture arrived at Hunstanton Secondary School, Norfolk (1949–54), by Peter and Alison Smithson. An example of what became known as the New Brutalism, this building was influenced by Mies van der Rohe. Most New Brutalist buildings, however, owed more to Le Corbusier's late work—for example, the gray concrete masses of Denys Lasdun's University of East Anglia, Norfolk (1962–68)—while Sir James Stirling's History Faculty, Cambridge (1964–67), brought a neo-Constructivist element to the Brutalist tradition. Canada gained the Central Technical School Arts Center by Robert Fairfield Associates (1964) and Scarborough College by John Andrews, with Page and Steele (1966), both in Toronto. Italian innovative educational architecture is exemplified in Milan's Instituto Marchiondi (1959) by Vittoriano Viganò.

Some of the new educational settings proposed solutions to what was undoubtedly the mid-20th century's greatest problem, its urban environment. The high-rise, dense campus at Boston University by José Luis Sert and

the skyscraper towers of MIT's earth-sciences
building (1964) by I.M. Pei, were imaginative
single buildings responding to urban circumstances. The Air Force Academy in Colorado
Springs, Colorado, and the Chicago campus
of the University of Illinois (1965), both by the
firm of Skidmore, Owings & Merrill with Walter
A. Netsch as the principal designer (1956),
and the Salk Institute for Biological Studies at
La Jolla, California, by Louis I. Kahn (1966), all
offered intimations of a new city built around a
cultural, educational centre.

No comparable concentration of intensive, harmonious urban architecture was
achieved for cities, even though after 1955
the building of new cities produced some
remarkable examples, such as Vällingby, Sweden; Brasília, the new capital of Brazil; and
Cumbernauld, in Scotland; and some remarkable renovations of old cities, as in Eastwicks
in Philadelphia (Reynolds Metals Co.; plans by
Constantinos Doxiadis, 1960) and Constitution
Plaza in Hartford, Connecticut (e.g., Charles
DuBose, with Sasaki, Walker & Associates
1964), and New York's Lincoln Center for the
Performing Arts (1962). By this time, however, it
was beginning to be felt that the application
of Modernist principles had caused visual
damage to historic cities and had also failed
to create a humane environment in new
cities. It was at this moment that the postmodernist era began.

POSTMODERNISM

In the 1960s some modification of the prevailing attitudes toward design of the previous 50 years began to take place. There was a revival of interest in traditional forms and historical styles. The American architect Louis Kahn reacted to the abstraction in the works of Le Corbusier and Mies by using regular geometric compositions and materials such as brick, stone, and wood that made reference to the spirit of some of the architecture from the past, especially Egyptian, Greek, and Roman. Other architects rejected International Style modernism in more literal ways, using past forms like Classical columns or drawing on the architecture of modern popular culture, the highway, and the suburb for inspiration. This artistic experimentation has run parallel to the explosion of construction for purely practical purposes.

The 1960s were marked by dissatisfaction with the consequences of the Modernist movement, especially in North America, where its failings were exposed in two influential books, Canadian Jane Jacobs's *The Death and Life of Great American Cities* (1961) and American Robert Venturi's *Complexity and Contradiction in Architecture* (1966). Jacobs criticized the destruction of urban coherence that was wrought by the presence of Modernist buildings, while Venturi implied that Modernist buildings were without meaning, as their puritanical design lacked the irony and complexity that enrich historical architecture. This dissatisfaction was translated into direct action in 1972 with the demolition of several 14-story slab blocks that had been built only 20 years earlier from designs by Minoru Yamasaki as part of the award-winning Pruitt-Igoe housing development in St. Louis, Missouri. Similar apartment blocks in Europe and North America were demolished in the following decades, but it was in St. Louis that the post-modernist era was begun.

Despite this backlash, many established corporations continued to commission clean-lined Modernist towers to represent their corporate identity; indeed, the Modernist formal language, which had once seemed revolutionary, was often diluted to a bland austerity that came to represent industry in the late 20th century. In the early 1970s, American business was represented by the world's tallest structures at the time. The twin towers of the World Trade Center, designed by Yamasaki, opened in New York City in 1972. These stark, puritanical structures were for a time the tallest buildings in the world, until they were surpassed one year later by Chicago's enormous Sears (now Willis) Tower, designed by engineer Fazlur Khan. Such structures would face increasing criticism with the advent of postmodernism. (A different, more tragic challenge to this philosophy of architecture would come decades later as a result of the terrorist attacks on the World Trade Center in 2001, which further caused architects to rethink the longstanding connection between industry and imposing, Modernist-derived structures.)

Concurrent with the building of these skyscrapers, Venturi's *Learning from Las Vegas* (with Denise Scott Brown and Steven Izenour) was published in 1972. In seeking to rehumanize

architecture by ridding it of the restricting purism of Modernism, the authors pointed to the
playful commercial architecture and billboards
of the Las Vegas highways for guidance. Venturi
and his partner John Rauch reintroduced to
architectural design elements of wit, humanity,
and historical reference in buildings such as
the Tucker House in Katonah, New York (1975).
Many architects in the 1970s and '80s followed
this lead and adopted a populist language

The twin towers of the World Trade Center *(left)* were destroyed in the
terrorist attacks of September 11, 2001. The same area of New York City
after the attacks is shown with a dramatically altered skyline *(right)*.

scattered with Classical souvenirs. For example, Philip Johnson and his partner John Burgee designed the AT&T Building in New York City (1978–84), a skyscraper with a Chippendale skyline. Similarly, Michael Graves's Portland Public Service Building in Portland, Oregon (1980–82), has the bulk of the modern sky-scraper yet incorporates historical souvenirs such as the colonnade, belvedere, keystone, and swag. Like Charles Moore's Piazza d'Italia in New Orleans (1975–80) and Alumni Center at the University of California at Irvine (1983–85), these confident and colourful buildings were intended to reassure the public that it need no longer feel that its cultural identity is threatened by modern architecture. This mood was encap-sulated in Venice in 1980 when a varied group of American and European architects, includ-ing Venturi, Charles Moore, Paolo Portoghesi, Aldo Rossi, Hans Hollein, Ricardo Bofill, and Léon Krier, provided designs for an exhibition orga-nized by the Venice Biennale under the title, "The Presence of the Past." These key architects of postmodernism represented several different outlooks but shared a desire to banish the fear of memory from modern architectural design.

Postmodernist experimentation was often overtly ironic. For example, the Centre Georges Pompidou in Paris (1971–77), by Renzo Piano and Richard Rogers, with its services and struc-ture exposed externally and painted in primary colours, can be seen as an outrageous joke in the historic centre of Paris. The building has a postmodernist flavour: it playfully acknowledges the historical belief, going back at least to Eugène-Emmanuel Viollet-le-Duc and continuing through Modernism, in the truthful exposure

The postmodernist Pompidou Centre, in Paris, France, was designed by architects Renzo Piano and Richard Rogers and completed in 1977.

of the structural bones of a building. Rogers repeated the theme in his Lloyd's Building in London (1984–86). Sir James Stirling's addition to the Staatsgalerie in Stuttgart, Germany (1977–82), also a key postmodernist building, makes ironic references to the language of Karl Friedrich Schinkel without accepting the fundamental principles of Classicism.

Rejecting the playful elements in such buildings as kitsch, some architects, notably Allan Greenberg and John Blatteau, chose a more historically faithful Classical style, as in their official reception rooms of the United States Department of State in Washington, D.C. (1984–85). Undeviating Classicism was pursued in Britain by, among others, Quinlan Terry (Riverside Development, Richmond, Surrey, 1986–88). Along the same lines, Krier was influential in both the United States and Britain for his iconlike drawings of city planning schemes in a ruthlessly simple Classical style and for his polemical attacks on what he saw as modern technology's destruction of civic order and human dignity. The spirit of Classical urban renewal was represented in France by Bofill's vast housing developments, such as Les Espaces d'Abraxas in Marne-la-Vallée, near Paris (1978–83). The gargantuan scale of this columnar architecture of prefabricated concrete pushed the language of Classicism to its limits and beyond.

Many architectural critics have observed that postmodern architecture was characterized by superficiality, excess, and derivation. But, rather than being superficial in their love of cartoonlike, over-scaled Classical forms and details, many postmodern architects were seriously attempting to place their creations within historic as well as local design contexts. Examples of this tendency range from Graves's Humana Building (1982) in Louisville, Kentucky, in which he consciously attempted to link this new classicist skyscraper to America's masonry skyscrapers from the early 20th century, to José Rafael Moneo's National Museum of Roman Art (1986) in Mérida, Spain, which features a sequence of simple, round brick arches that make reference to the ancient Roman tradition of arched-brick buildings.

Postmodernism nonetheless faded from favour at the end of the 20th century. Contextual efforts continued through the 1990s, but often with a renewed appreciation of Modernist principles. This increasing appreciation for the simple lines of Modernist buildings perhaps related to the leaner recession years of the early 1990s that developed after "black Monday," the stock market crash of October 19, 1987. Terms such as "value engineered" became commonplace in the 1990s, denoting that clients wished to save money through simpler, streamlined designs, making the elaborate, costly ornamentation associated with postmodernism increasingly irrelevant as the millennium approached.

While office vacancy rates began to climb in the United States and Europe, international architects worked on rebuilding cities in China and Southeast Asia until the recession eventually spread there. Prominent buildings illustrating the newfound importance of that region include Cesar Pelli's Petronas Twin Towers (1992–98) in Kuala Lumpur, Malaysia—which surpassed the Sears Tower (later [from 2009] Willis Tower) as the tallest building in the world at 1,483 feet (452 metres) high—and Skidmore, Owings & Merrill's Jin Mao Tower (1999), in Shanghai, China's tallest building, which stands at 1,380 feet (420 metres). Although neither is as overtly historicist as slightly earlier postmodern buildings, both have contextual references to their respective environments: the plans of the Petronas Towers use Islamic design motifs, and the design of Jin Mao Tower makes conscious reference to Chinese pagoda forms.

DECONSTRUCTION

While some architects in the 1990s continued to design buildings with contextual elements, others strove to make a clean break with the overt historicism of postmodernism. The

Museum of Modern Art's exhibition "Deconstructivist Architecture" (1988) included a number of architects whose angular spatial compositions appear to be tangible realizations of chaos theory, but which are also in many ways reminiscent of Russian Constructivist and German Expressionist architectural forms from the early 1920s. Architects such as Wolf Prix and Helmut Swiczinsky of the Austrian firm of Coop Himmelblau demonstrated this individualistic, dynamic juxtaposition of forms in buildings such as the Funder Factory Works (1988) in St. Veit, Austria, and the offices atop Falkestrasse 6 (1983–88) in Vienna. An almost violent, disruptive placement of angular rectilinear forms and spaces often appeared in similar works of architecture that can be termed "deconstructivist" architecture, a movement related to the literary theory of the same name. Examples of deconstructivist architecture include Daniel Libeskind's Jewish Museum in Berlin (1989–99); Zaha Hadid's Vitra Fire Station in Weil am Rhein, Germany (1989–93), and her "Mind Zone" exhibition within Richard Rogers's Millennium Dome in Greenwich, England (1999); and Peter Eisenman's Wexner Center for the Visual Arts in Columbus, Ohio (1983–89). Rem Koolhaas's work shares many of the same qualities as the work of these architects, although he is probably known more for his architectural writings, such as *Delirious New York* (1978) and *S,M,L,XL* (1996), than for his buildings.

MILLENNIAL TRENDS

The 1990s witnessed two remarkable architectural events that helped revitalize existing architectural environments. The first of these came with the fall of the Berlin Wall on November 9, 1989, and the subsequent reunification of Germany. After selecting Berlin as the capital of a new Germany, the government held numerous architectural competitions for various buildings and neighbourhoods throughout the city. Of all of them, perhaps the most important was that for Potsdamer Platz, the former no-man's land between East and West Berlin and the centre of the new city. Held in 1991, the competition resulted in buildings being constructed over the next decade and more. This new city centre contained showpiece buildings by international architects such Renzo Piano, Richard Rogers, Rafael Moneo, and Helmut Jahn.

The second significant event of the 1990s was the revitalization of the industrial city of Bilbao, Spain, which used architecture as a central way to redefine itself. Some of the architects selected for projects there included international figures such as Sir Norman Foster, Santiago Calatrava, Robert A.M. Stern, and Ricardo Legorreta. The city's most famous work, however, was by Frank Gehry. Other cities in Europe and Asia in the 1980s held international competitions to revitalize various urban neighbourhoods

FRANK O. GEHRY

Frank O. Gehry (b. February 28, 1929, Toronto, Ontario, Canada) immigrated to Los Angeles from Canada in 1947. Gehry studied architecture at the University of Southern California (1949–51; 1954) and city planning at Harvard University (1956–57). After working for several architectural firms, he established his own company, Frank O. Gehry & Associates, in 1962 and established its successor, Gehry Partners, in 2002.

Reacting, like many of his contemporaries, against the cold and often formulaic Modernist buildings that had begun to dot many cityscapes, Gehry began to experiment with unusual expressive devices and to search for a personal vocabulary. In his early work he built unique, quirky structures that emphasized human scale and contextual integrity. His early experiments are perhaps best embodied by the "renovations" he made to his own home (1978, 1991–94) in Santa Monica, California. Gehry essentially stripped the two-story home down to its frame and then built a chain-link and corrugated-steel frame around it, complete with asymmetrical protrusions of steel rod and glass. Gehry made the traditional bungalow—and the

(continued on the next page)

(continued from the previous page)

architectural norms it embodied—appear to have exploded wide open. He continued those design experiments in two popular lines of corrugated cardboard furniture, **Easy Edges** (1969-73) and **Experimental Edges** (1979-82). Gehry's ability to undermine the viewer's expectations of traditional materials and forms led him to be grouped with the deconstructivist movement in architecture, although his play upon architectural tradition also caused him to be linked to postmodernism.

Treating each new commission as "a sculptural object, a spatial container, a space with light and air," Gehry was rewarded with commissions the world over throughout the 1980s and '90s. These works possessed the deconstructed quality of his Santa Monica home but began to display a pristine grandeur that suited his increasingly public projects. Notable structures from the period include the Vitra Furniture Museum and Factory (1987) in Weil am Rhein, Germany; the American Center (1988-94) in Paris; and the Frederick R. Weisman Art Museum (1990-93) at the University of Minnesota in Minneapolis.

Gehry's reputation soared in the late 1990s. By that time Gehry's trademark style had become buildings that resemble undulating free-form sculpture. This form

arguably reached its zenith in his Guggenheim Museum (1991–97) in Bilbao, Spain. In
that structure Gehry combined curvaceous
titanium forms with interconnecting limestone masses to create a sculptural feat of
engineering. He further explored those concerns in the Experience Music Project (1995–
2000) in Seattle. Constructed of a fabricated
steel frame wrapped in colourful sheet metal,
the structure was, according to Gehry, modeled on the shape of a guitar—particularly,
a smashed electric guitar. As with the
Guggenheim structure, he employed cutting-
edge computer technology to uncover the
engineering solutions that could bring his
sculptural sketches to life. In his 2008 renovation of the Art Museum of Ontario in his
hometown, Gehry retained the original
building (1918) but removed an artistically
unsuccessful entryway that had been added
in the 1990s. Although the updated museum
shows many characteristic Gehry touches,
one critic called it "one of Mr. Gehry's most
gentle and self-possessed designs."

Gehry became known for his work on
music venues. The Walt Disney Concert Hall
in Los Angeles was designed before the Bilbao museum but was completed in 2003,
to great acclaim. The Jay Pritzker Pavilion in
Chicago's Millennium Park was completed in

(continued on the next page)

(continued from the previous page)

2004. Gehry also built a performing arts centre (1997–2003) for Bard College in Annandale-on-Hudson, New York, and designed the New World Center (completed 2011) for the New World Symphony orchestral academy in Miami Beach, Florida. As the 21st century progressed, Gehry continued to receive numerous large-scale commissions.

Although critical opinion is sometimes divided over his radical structures, Gehry's work made architecture popular and talked-about in a manner not seen in the United States since Frank Lloyd Wright. Among Gehry's many awards are the Pritzker Architecture Prize (1989), the National Medal of the Arts (1998), and the American Institute of Architects Gold Medal (1999).

(e.g., Berlin and Frankfurt, in Germany, and Nara and Fukuoka, in Japan), but Bilbao distinguished itself by making a deliberate effort to put itself on the world's cultural map with the construction of a branch of the Guggenheim Museum (1991–97) designed by Gehry. Upon its opening, the building became an international success. Its angular, anthropomorphic exterior, made mostly of titanium, made reference to the industrial heritage of this city's former shipyards while also providing a dynamic new image for Bilbao.

Gehry generally works from numerous architectural models when he plans his buildings, but he actualized the individualistic shapes of the Guggenheim through the use of computer-generated forms that facilitated the planning and engineering of the structure. Computer technology helped to bring about many such major architectural advancements at the turn of the 21st century. Even though firms such as Skidmore, Owings & Merrill pioneered the use of computers for architectural and engineering design in the early to mid-1980s, using them to create architectural renderings as early as 1985, the personal computer did not see widespread use in small and large architectural offices until the mid-1990s, when it became a ubiquitous design tool in almost every architectural firm. Younger firms such as Diller and Scofidio, Garofalo Architects, and Greg Lynn were able to make highly expressive, curvilinear structures and spaces because of this electronic tool. Gehry went on to use the CATIA system, a program used in aerospace engineering, to design his anthropomorphic, wildly expressive Experience Music Project (completed 2000) in Seattle. In addition to using new technology to create the ultimate in an expressionist, modern aesthetic, architects also used technical advancements such as energy-efficient, double-glass walls and louvered facades to create sustainable buildings that were environmentally friendly. Architects such as Foster

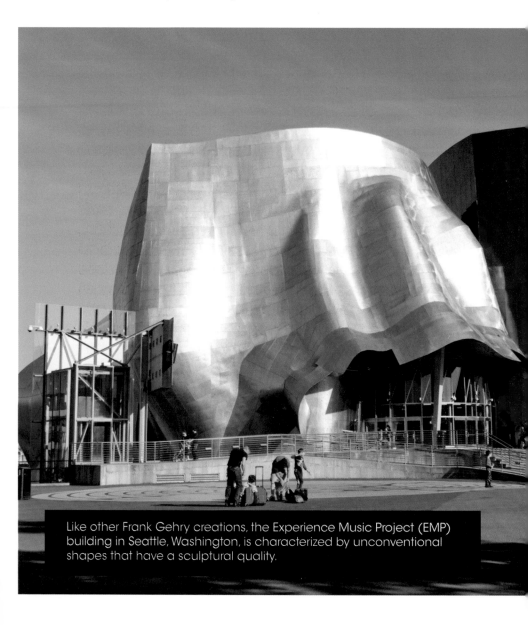

Like other Frank Gehry creations, the Experience Music Project (EMP) building in Seattle, Washington, is characterized by unconventional shapes that have a sculptural quality.

and Ken Yeang became well-respected specialists in this pursuit, utilizing sun and shade to their best advantage in their buildings, and planting trees within internal atria that were, as the rest of the building, naturally ventilated.

One tendency that linked postmodernism, deconstruction, and most trends at the turn of the 21st century was the international star system. In 1979 the Pritzker Architecture Prize was established by the Hyatt Foundation in Chicago. This prestigious award, likened to the Nobel Prize for architecture, spawned several other international architectural awards, such as the Praemeum Imperiale in Japan (1988) and the Carlsberg Prize in Denmark (1992). The Pritzker Prize's laureate list reads like a "who's who" of contemporary architecture.

Past winners represent many architectural stylistic preferences and many nations, from the then-postmodern practitioners Philip Johnson (1979; American), Sir James Stirling (1981; British), and Hans Hollein (1985; Austrian) to deconstructivists such as Gehry (1989; Canadian-born American) and Koolhaas (2000; Dutch), Minimalists such as Álvaro Siza (1992; Portuguese) and Tadao Ando (1995; Japanese), and technology-savvy designers such as Renzo Piano (1998; Italian) and Sir Norman Foster (1999; British). The Pritzker Prize became as much a part of American and international social history as a part of architectural history: just as novelists, actors, and pop singers captured intense media attention in the late 20th century, these celebrity "starchitects," as they have been called, received widespread attention through international exhibitions, lectures, design magazines, and monographs. At the turn of the 21st century these superstars made their marks all over the world, and stylistic categorization gave way to the unique visions of the individual architects.

As a result of the growing interest in architecture as environment, three design professions—architecture, landscape architecture, and urban design—in 2011 began collaborating with one another more than they had in the recent past. Often they worked as equals on large projects. Some designers called themselves "landscape urbanists," thus merging two of the disciplines. Other architects, believing that architecture should embody a strong social purpose, designed affordable housing for areas devastated by climate disasters.

Iraqi-born British architect Zaha Hadid is known for her radical deconstructivist designs. In 2004 she became the first woman to be awarded the Pritzker Prize. In 2010 Hadid's boldly imaginative design for the MAXXI museum of contemporary art and architecture in Rome earned her the Royal Institute of British Architects (RIBA) Stirling Prize for the best building by a British architect completed in the past year. She won a second Stirling Prize the following year for a sleek structure she conceived for Evelyn Grace Academy, a secondary school in London. Hadid's fluid undulating design for the Heydar Aliyev Center, a cultural centre that opened in 2012 in Baku, Azerbaijan, won the London Design Museum's Design of the Year in 2014. She was the first woman to earn that award—which judges designs in architecture, furniture, fashion, graphics, product, and transportation—and the design was the first from the architecture category. Her other notable works include the London Aquatics Centre built for the 2012 Olympics and the Eli and Edythe Broad Art Museum, which opened in 2012 at Michigan State University in East Lansing, Michigan.

American architect Jeanne Gang is known for her innovative responses to issues of environmental and ecological sustainability. She employed sustainable-design techniques—such as the use of recycled materials—to conserve resources, decrease urban sprawl, and increase biodiversity. She is perhaps best known for her Aqua Tower, an 82-story mixed-use skyscraper in downtown Chicago that, when completed in 2010, was one of the tallest buildings in the world designed by a woman. Gang's firm participated in the Venice Biennale in 2004 and 2012 and received the Emporis Award in 2009 for the best new skyscraper of the year. In 2006 Gang received the Arts and Letters Award in Architecture from the American Academy of Arts and Letters, and she was awarded a MacArthur Foundation "genius grant" in 2011. In 2013 Studio Gang Architects received the Architecture Design Award—awarded to an individual or a firm for "exceptional exemplary work in public, commercial, or residential architectural design"—from Cooper-Hewitt, National Design Museum.

Portuguese architect Eduardo Souto de Moura, who was commended for integrating the clean lines of minimalism with such nonminimal elements as colour and the use of local materials, in 2011 won the Pritzker Prize. The prize jury cited the "intelligence and seriousness" of his work and noted that his architecture "appears effortless, serene, and simple."

On September 17, 2013, British architect Sir David Chipperfield was announced as the architectural laureate of the Praemium Imperiale 2013. The award, granted annually by the Japan Association, was in recognition of Chipperfield's "modest, thoughtful art form. ... With an unerring eye for elegant diffuse and natural lighting, his designs reveal a building's essential quality in a graceful and quiet atmosphere." One of Chipperfield's most recent commissions, the East Building of the Saint Louis (Missouri) Art Museum, provided an ideal expression of that sentiment. The light-filled East Building boasted skylights, floor-to-ceiling windows on the front, a concrete facade that was composed of locally sourced river aggregates, and a Gold LEED rating from the U.S. Green Building Council. Two other buildings designed by his firm, David Chipperfield Architects, were also completed in 2013: the Europaallee 21 office building in Zürich (July) and the Museo Jumex in Mexico City (November).

GREEN ARCHITECTURE

Green architecture is the philosophy of architecture that advocates sustainable energy sources, the conservation of energy, the reuse and safety of building materials, and the siting of a building with consideration of its impact on the environment.

In the early 21st century the building of shelter (in all its forms) consumed more than half of the world's resources—translating into 16 percent of the Earth's freshwater resources, 30–40 percent of all energy supplies, and 50 percent by weight of all the raw materials withdrawn from Earth's surface. Architecture was also responsible for 40–50 percent of waste deposits in landfills and 20–30 percent of greenhouse gas emissions.

Many architects after the post-World War II building boom were content to erect emblematic civic and corporate icons that celebrated profligate consumption and omnivorous globalization. At the turn of the 21st century, however, a building's environmental integrity—as seen in the way it was designed and how it operated—became an important factor in how it was evaluated.

By the mid-1980s and continuing through the '90s, the number of environmental advocacy societies radically expanded; groups such as Greenpeace, Environmental Action, the Sierra Club, Friends of the Earth, and the Nature Conservancy all experienced burgeoning memberships. For architects and builders a significant milestone was the formulation in 1994 of Leadership in Energy and Environmental Design (LEED) standards, established and administered by the U.S. Green Building

Council. These standards provided measurable criteria for the design and construction of environmentally responsible buildings.

The 1980s and early '90s brought a new surge of interest in the environmental movement and the rise to prominence of a group of more socially responsive and philosophically oriented green architects. The American architect Malcolm Wells opposed the legacy of architectural ostentation and aggressive assaults on the land in favour of the gentle impact of underground and earth-sheltered buildings—exemplified by his Brewster, Massachusetts, house of 1980. The low impact, in both energy use and visual effect, of a structure that is surrounded by earth creates an almost invisible architecture and a green ideal. As Wells explained, this kind of underground building is "sunny, dry, and pleasant" and "offers huge fuel savings and a silent, green alternative to the asphalt society."

The American architect William McDonough rose to green design fame in 1985 with his Environmental Defense Fund Building in New York City. That structure was one of the first civic icons for energy conservation resulting from the architect's close scrutiny of all of its interior products, construction technology, and air-handling systems. Since then, McDonough's firm established valuable planning strategies and built numerous other green buildings—most significantly, the Herman Miller factory and offices (Holland, Michigan, 1995), the corporate offices of Gap, Inc. (San Bruno, California, 1997), and Oberlin College's Adam Joseph Lewis Center for Environmental Studies (Oberlin, Ohio, 2001).

McDonough's main contribution to the evolution of sustainable design was his commitment to what he has called "ecologically intelligent design," a process that involves the cooperation of the architect, corporate leaders, and scientists. This design principle

Among other revolutionary features, the Adam Joseph Lewis Center for Environmental Studies at Oberlin College is capable of producing more energy than it consumes, using the excess energy for other needs in the community.

takes into account the "biography" of every aspect of manufacture, use, and disposal: the choice of raw ingredients, transport of materials to the factory, fabrication process, durability of goods produced, usability of products, and recycling potential. McDonough's latest version of the principle—referred to as "cradle-to-cradle" design—is modeled after nature's own waste-free economy and makes a strong case for the goal of reprocessing, in which every element that is used in or that results from the manufacturing process has its own built-in recycling value.

If architecture is to become truly green, then a revolution of form and content—including radical changes in the entire look of architecture—is essential. This can only happen if those involved in the building arts create a fundamentally new language that is more contextually integrative, socially responsive, functionally ethical, and visually germane.

The potentialities of environmental science and technology must be creatively examined. Already there exists a rich reservoir of ideas from science and nature—cybernetics, virtual reality, biochemistry, hydrology, geology, and cosmology, to mention a few. Furthermore, just as the Industrial Revolution once generated change in many fields in the 19th century, so too the information revolution, with its model of integrated systems, serves as a conceptual model in the

21st century for a new approach to architecture and design in the broader environment.

As community governments begin to legislate state-of-the-art green standards, they must encourage appropriate artistic responses to such regional attributes as surrounding topography, indigenous vegetation, cultural history, and territorial idiosyncrasy. For instance, communities might encourage innovative fusions of architecture with landscape—where trees and plants become as much a part of architectural design as construction materials—so that buildings and their adjacent landscapes essentially merge. In such thinking, buildings are not interpreted as isolated objects, and the traditional barriers between inside and outside and between structure and site are challenged.

Likewise, green architecture in the 21st century has similar obligations to the psychological and physical needs of its inhabitants. Buildings are most successful when they respond to multiple senses—meaning that truly green design engages touch, smell, and hearing as well as sight in the design of buildings and public spaces.

Continuing advances in environmental technology have significantly strengthened the goals of sustainable architecture and city planning over the last decade. Yet many people consider the environmental crisis beyond their comprehension and control.

Though technological solutions are necessary, they represent only one facet of the whole. Indeed, the transfer of responsibility to engineers and scientists threatens the social and psychological commitment needed for philosophical unity.

Increasing numbers of people seek new symbiotic relationships between their shelter and the broader ecology. This growing motivation is one of the most promising signs in the development of a consensus philosophy of the environment.

The types of architecture are established not by architects but by society, according to the needs of its different institutions. Society sets the goals and assigns to the architect the job of finding the means of achieving them.

The history of Western architecture is marked by a series of new solutions to structural problems. During the period from the beginning of civilization through ancient Greek culture, construction methods progressed from the most primitive shed roof and simple truss to the vertical posts, or columns, supporting horizontal beams, or lintels. Greek architecture also formalized many structural and decorative elements into three Classical orders—Ionic, Doric, and Corinthian—which, to a greater or lesser extent, have influenced architecture since that time. The Romans exploited the arch, vault, and dome and made broader use of the load-bearing masonry wall. In the late medieval period, the pointed arch, ribbing, and pier systems gradually emerged. At this point all the problems of brick and stone masonry construction had been solved, and, beyond decorative advances, little innovation was achieved until the Industrial Revolution.

Not until the 19th century, with the advent of cast-iron and steel construction, did a new architectural age dawn and higher, broader, and lighter buildings become possible. With the advances of 20th-century technology, new structural methods such as cantilevering received more extensive use. By the turn of the 21st century, computers had further enhanced architects' ability to conceptualize and create new forms.

The practice of architecture is employed to fulfill both practical and expressive requirements, and thus it serves both utilitarian and aesthetic ends. Although these two ends may be distinguished, they cannot be separated, and the relative weight given to each can vary widely. Because every society—whether highly developed or less so, settled or nomadic—has a spatial relationship to the natural world and to other societies, the structures they produce reveal much about their environment (including climate and weather), history, ceremonies, and artistic sensibility, as well as the varied aspects of daily life.

GLOSSARY

acropolis A central, defensively oriented district in ancient Greek cities, located on the highest ground and containing the chief municipal and religious buildings.

aqueduct A conduit built to carry water from its source to a main distribution point.

arabesque A style of decoration characterized by interlacing plant forms and abstract curvilinear motifs.

architrave The lowest division of an entablature resting in classical architecture immediately on the capital of the column.

basilica Originally a secular public building in ancient Rome, typically a large rectangular structure with an open hall and a raised platform at one or both ends. The early Christians adopted this type for their churches, which consisted of a nave and aisles with clerestory and a large high transept from which an apse projects.

buttress An exterior support, usually of masonry, projecting from the face of a wall and serving to strengthen it or resist outward thrust from an arch or roof.

calefactory A monastery room warmed and used as a sitting room.

cantilever A long beam of wood, metal, etc., that projects from a wall or other structure to support something above it (such as a balcony or bridge).

cella The frequently hidden inner part of a Greek or Roman temple that housed the image of the deity.

chevet The apsidal eastern termination of a church choir typically having a surrounding ambulatory that opens onto a number of radiating apses or chapels.

cistern An underground container that is used for collecting and storing rainwater.

clerestory An outside wall of a room or building (as a church) carried above an adjoining roof and pierced with windows which admit light to the interior.

coffer A recessed panel, usually with other panels forming a continuous pattern in a vault, ceiling, or soffit.

cornice The decorative top edge of a building or column.

dolmen A prehistoric monument of two or more upright stones supporting a horizontal stone slab found especially in Britain and France and thought to be a tomb.

entablature An assemblage of horizontal moldings and bands supported by the columns of Classical buildings.

entasis A convex curve given to a column, spire, or similar upright member to avoid the optical illusion of hollowness or weakness that would arise from normal tapering.

frieze A horizontal band, often decorated with relief sculpture, between the architrave and cornice of a building.

hippodrome An oval stadium for horse and chariot races in ancient Greece.

Iconoclastic Controversy A dispute over the use of religious images (icons) in the Byzantine Empire in the 8th and 9th centuries. The Iconoclasts (those who rejected images) objected to icon worship for several reasons, including the Old Testament prohibition against images in the Ten Commandments (Ex. 20:4) and the possibility of idolatry. The defenders of icon worship insisted on the symbolic nature of images and on the dignity of created matter.

insula An ancient Roman building or a group of buildings standing together forming a block or square and usually constituting an apartment building.

lintel A piece of wood or stone that lies across the top of a door or window and holds the weight of the structure above it.

loggia A roofed open gallery especially at an upper story overlooking an open court.

mastaba A rectangular superstructure of ancient Egyptian tombs, built of mud brick or, later, stone, with sloping walls and a flat roof.

menhir A single upright rough monolith usually of prehistoric origin.

metope The space between two triglyphs of a Doric frieze often adorned with carved work.

order Any of several styles defined by the particular type of column, base, capital, and entablature they use.

pediment A triangular space that forms the gable of a low-pitched roof and that is usually filled with relief sculpture in classical architecture.

pendentive One of the concave triangular members that support a dome over a square space.

peristyle A colonnade surrounding a building or court.

pilaster An upright architectural member that is rectangular in plan and is structurally a pier but architecturally treated as a column and that usually projects a third of its width or less from the wall.

post-and-beam system In building construction, a system in which two upright members, the posts, hold up a third member, the beam, laid horizontally across their top surfaces. In

Britain it is called post-and-lintel system, but in the United States "lintel" is usually reserved for a short beam that spans a window or door opening.

pozzolana Finely divided siliceous or siliceous and aluminous material that reacts chemically with slaked lime at ordinary temperature and in the presence of moisture to form a strong slow-hardening cement.

refectory A dining hall in a monastery, convent, or religious college.

rustication Masonry having the surface textured, reticulated, or otherwise accented or the joints emphasized.

squinch A support (as an arch, lintel, or corbeling) carried across the corner of a room under a superimposed mass.

stylobate A continuous flat pavement on which a row of columns is supported.

tracery Bars or ribs used decoratively in windows, especially the ornamental openwork in Gothic windows.

transept The shorter area that goes across and sticks out from the long part of a church and that gives the church the shape of a cross when it is viewed from above.

triforium A gallery or open space forming an upper story to the aisle of a church and typically constituting an arcaded story between the nave arches and clerestory.

triglyph A slightly projecting rectangular tablet in a Doric frieze with two vertical channels of a V section and two corresponding chamfers or half channels on the vertical sides.

volute A spiral scroll-shaped ornament forming the chief feature of the Ionic capital.

ziggurat An ancient Mesopotamian temple tower consisting of a lofty pyramidal structure built in successive stages with outside staircases and a shrine at the top.

BIBLIOGRAPHY

CLASSICAL GREEK AND HELLENISTIC

Major surveys are offered in William Bell Dinsmoor, *The Architecture of Ancient Greece: An Account of Its Historic Development*, 3rd ed. rev. (1950, reprinted 1975); A.W. Lawrence, *Greek Architecture*, 5th ed., rev. by R.A. Tomlinson (1996); J.J. Coulton, *Ancient Greek Architects at Work: Problems of Structure and Design* (1977, reissued 1991; also published as *Greek Architects at Work*, 1977, reprinted 1982); J.J. Pollitt, *The Art of Ancient Greece: Sources and Documents*, rev. ed. (1990, reprinted 1995), and *Art in the Hellenistic Age* (1986, reissued 1996); and James Steele and Ersin Alok, *Hellenistic Architecture in Asia Minor* (1992).

ROMAN

The basic source is Vitruvius, *The Ten Books on Architecture*, trans. from Latin by Morris Hicky Morgan (1914, reprinted 1960), the only complete treatise to survive from antiquity. Authoritative surveys with informative bibliographies are Axel Boëthius, *Etruscan and*

Early Roman Architecture, 2nd ed., rev. by Roger Ling and Tom Rasmussen (1994); and J.B. Ward-Perkins, *Roman Imperial Architecture* (1981, reissued 1994). Also of interest are William L. MacDonald, *The Architecture of the Roman Empire*, rev. ed., 2 vol. (1982–86); Margaret Lyttelton, *Baroque Architecture in Classical Antiquity* (1974); and J.J. Pollitt, *The Art of Rome, c. 753 B.C.–337 A.D.: Sources and Documents* (1966, reprinted 1983).

EARLY CHRISTIAN AND BYZANTINE

Richard Krautheimer, *Early Christian and Byzantine Architecture*, 4th ed., rev. by Richard Krautheimer and Slobodan Curcic (1986), is a major study. Also informative is E. Baldwin Smith, *Architectural Symbolism of Imperial Rome and the Middle Ages* (1956, reprinted 1978). Constantinople (Istanbul) is covered in Thomas F. Mathews, *The Byzantine Churches of Istanbul: A Photographic Survey* (1976). Hubert Faensen, Vladimir Ivanov, and Klaus G. Beyer, *Early Russian Architecture* (1975; originally published in German, 1972), is a useful introduction.

EARLY MEDIEVAL AND ROMANESQUE

The fundamental study is Kenneth John Conant, *Carolingian and Romanesque Architecture, 800 to 1200*, 3rd ed. (1973). Also of interest are Eric Fernie, *The Architecture of the Anglo-Saxons* (1983), and *The Architecture of Norman England* (2000); Rolf Toman (ed.), *Romanesque: Architecture, Sculpture, Painting* (1997; originally published in German, 1996); and Roger Stalley, *Early Medieval Architecture* (1999).

GOTHIC

Paul Frankl, *Gothic Architecture*, rev. ed. by Paul Crossley (2001), provides a full scholarly survey. Earlier classics include Otto Von Simson, *The Gothic Cathedral: Origins of Gothic Architecture and the Medieval Concept of Order*, 3rd expanded ed. (1988); and Erwin Panofsky, *Gothic Architecture and Scholasticism* (1951, reissued 1985); also see Jean Bony, *The English Decorated Style: Gothic Architecture Transformed, 1250–1350* (1979); and Rolf Toman (ed.), *The Art of Gothic: Architecture, Sculpture, Painting* (1999; originally published in German, 1998). Also useful is Teresa G. Frisch, *Gothic Art*

1140–c. 1450: Sources and Documents (1971, reissued 1987).

RENAISSANCE

The best general surveys of Italian Renaissance architecture are Ludwig H. Heydenreich, *Architecture in Italy, 1400–1500*, rev. by Paul Davies (1996); and Wolfgang Lotz, *Architecture in Italy, 1500–1600*, rev. by Deborah Howard (1995). Rudolf Wittkower, *Architectural Principles in the Age of Humanism*, 5th ed. (1998), a scholarly study, may be read in conjunction with historical treatises, especially Leon Battista Alberti, *On the Art of Building in Ten Books*, (1988, reprinted 1991; originally published in Latin, 1485); and Andrea Palladio, *The Four Books of Architecture* (1738, reprinted 1977; originally published in Italian, 1570).

Informative works on Renaissance architecture outside of Italy include Anthony Blunt, *Art and Architecture in France, 1500–1700*, 5th ed., rev. by Richard Beresford (1999); George Kubler and Martin Soria, *Art and Architecture in Spain and Portugal and Their American Dominions, 1500 to 1800* (1959, reissued 1969); John Summerson, *Architecture in Britain, 1530 to 1830*, 9th ed. (1993); and Helena Kozakiewiczowie and Stefan Kozakiewiczowie, *The Renaissance in Poland* (1976; originally published in Polish, 1976).

BAROQUE AND ROCOCO

Important general studies include Anthony Blunt (ed.), *Baroque & Rococo Architecture & Decoration* (1978, reprinted 1988). The classic study on Italian Baroque is Rudolf Wittkower, *Art and Architecture in Italy, 1600–1750*, rev. by Joseph Connors and Jennifer Montagu, 6th ed., 3 vol. (1999). Informative works on specific parts of Italy include Anthony Blunt, *Neapolitan Baroque & Rococo Architecture* (1975); and Richard Pommer, *Eighteenth-Century Architecture in Piedmont: The Open Structures of Juvarra, Alfieri & Vittone* (1967). Works dealing with the period's architecture elsewhere include Karsten Harries, *The Bavarian Rococo Church: Between Faith and Aestheticism* (1983); W. Kuyper, *Dutch Classicist Architecture: A Survey of Dutch Architecture, Gardens, and Anglo-Dutch Architectural Relations from 1625 to 1700* (1980); Kerry Downes, *English Baroque Architecture* (1966); Rolf Tolman (ed.), *Baroque: Architecture, Sculpture, Painting* (1998; originally published in German, 1997); and Henry A. Millon (ed.), *The Triumph of the Baroque: Architecture in Europe, 1600–1750* (1999).

CLASSICISM, 1750-1830

Stimulating general studies include Joseph Rykwert, *The First Moderns: The Architects of the Eighteenth Century* (1980, reissued 1983), and *On Adam's House in Paradise: The Idea of the Primitive Hut in Architectural History*, 2nd ed. (1981); and Robin Middleton and David Watkin, *Neoclassical and 19th Century Architecture* (1980, reissued in 2 vol., 1987; originally published in Italian, 1977). Special subjects are covered in Allan Braham, *The Architecture of the French Enlightenment* (1980, reissued 1989); Wolfgang Herrmann, *Laugier and Eighteenth Century French Theory* (1962, reissued 1985); David Watkin and Tilman Mellinghoff, *German Architecture and the Classical Ideal* (1987), a well-illustrated survey with a full bibliography; M. Il'ina and A. Aleksandrova, *Moscow Monuments of Architecture, 18th–the First Third of the Nineteenth Century*, 2 vol. (1975), with parallel English and Russian texts; William H. Pierson, Jr., *American Buildings and Their Architects: The Colonial and Neo-Classical Styles* (1970, reprinted 1986); Carl W. Condit, *American Building: Materials and Techniques from the First Colonial Settlements to the Present*, 2nd ed. (1982); Marcus Whiffen and Frederick Koeper, *American Architecture: 1607–1976* (1981, reprinted in 2 vol., 1984); Roger G. Kennedy, *Greek Revival America* (1989); Wend von Kalnein, *Architecture in France in the Eighteenth Century*, trans. from German (1995); and Barry Bergdoll, *European Architecture, 1750–1890* (2000).

GOTHIC REVIVAL

Paul Frankl, *The Gothic: Literary Sources and Interpretations Through Eight Centuries* (1969, reissued 1983), is a fundamental study. Georg Germann, *Gothic Revival in Europe and Britain: Sources, Influences, and Ideas*, trans. from German (1972), has an unusually broad perspective. Informative works on Britain include Charles L. Eastlake, *A History of the Gothic Revival*, 2nd ed., edited by J. Mordaunt Crook (1978), a basic text first published in 1872; George L. Hersey, *High Victorian Gothic: A Study in Associationism* (1972); and Chris Brooks, Gothic Revival (1999). The United States is the focus of Phoebe B. Stanton, *The Gothic Revival & American Church Architecture: An Episode in Taste, 1840–1856* (1968, reprinted 1997);

and William H. Pierson, Jr., *Technology and the Picturesque: The Corporate and the Early Gothic Styles* (1978, reissued 1986).

20TH CENTURY

IRON AND GLASS

Important sources include François Loyer, *Architecture of the Industrial Age, 1789–1914* (1983; originally published in French, 1983); Sigfried Giedion, *Mechanization Takes Command: A Contribution to Anonymous History* (1948, reissued 1970); Carroll L.V. Meeks, *The Railroad Station: An Architectural History* (1956, reissued 1995); and Carl W. Condit, *American Building Art: The Twentieth Century* (1961). Frank Russell (ed.), *Art Nouveau Architecture* (1979, reprinted 1986), is a comprehensive survey.

MODERN MOVEMENT AND AFTER

Early classic studies include Henry-Russell Hitchcock and Philip Johnson, *The International Style* (1932, reissued 1996); Nikolaus Pevsner, *Pioneers of Modern Design: From William Morris to Walter Gropius*, rev. ed. (1975, reissued 1991); and Reyner Banham, *Theory and Design in the First Machine Age,* 2nd ed. (1967, reprinted 1992). A broader exploration is available in Kenneth Frampton, *Modern Architecture: A Critical History*, 3rd ed., rev. and enlarged (1992, reissued 1997). Modern American architecture is discussed in William H. Jordy, *American Buildings and Their Architects: The Impact of European Modernism in the Mid-Twentieth Century* (1972, reprinted 1986); Jane Jacobs, *The Death and Life of Great American Cities* (1961, reissued 2000); and the work by Carl W. Condit cited in the section above. Postmodernism has been surveyed in Paolo Portoghesi, *Postmodern: The Architecture of the Post-Industrial Society* (1983; originally published in Italian, 1982); and Charles Jencks, *The Language of Post-Modern Architecture*, 6th rev. and enlarged ed. (1991). Also of interest are Robert A.M. Stern and Raymond W. Gastil, *Modern Classicism* (1988); and Andreas Papadakis and Harriet Watson (eds.), *New Classicism: Omnibus Volume* (1990).

Other developments in late 20th-century and early 21st-century architecture are examined in Philip Johnson and Mark Wigley, *Deconstructivist Architecture: The Museum of Modern Art, New York* (1988); Charles Jencks,

The New Moderns: From Late to Neo-Modernism (1990); Peter Noever (ed.), *Architecture in Transition: Between Deconstruction and New Modernism* (1991, reissued 1997); Hugh Pearman, *Contemporary World Architecture* (1998); Martha Thorne (ed.), *The Pritzker Architecture Prize: The First Twenty Years* (1999); John Zukowsky and Martha Thorne (eds.), *Skyscrapers: The New Millennium* (2000); James Wines, *Green Architecture* (2000, reissued 2008), ed. by Philip Jodidio; and Philip Jodidio, *Green Architecture Now!* (2013).

INDEX